D1268003

WILD WISDOM

A WARTHOG'S TALE

LAURADA BYERS

ART BY NATALIE HAYS STEWART

Proceeds from the sale of this book will benefit the students of the Russell Byers Charter School.
warthogproductions.com

WARTHOG
PRODUCTIONS

WILD WISDOM - A WARTHOG'S TALE

Text and Illustrations Copyright © 2019 Warthog Productions

All rights reserved, including the right of reproduction in whole or in part in any form.

To order or purchase in bulk, please contact Laurada Byers at warthogproductions.com

Cover Design: Natalie Hays Stewart

Book Design: Natalie Hays Stewart

Layout: Stewart A. Williams

ISBN: 978-1-7324665-1-7

To Russell,

1940 - 1999

Lover...father...eggbeater...best friend

&

To the students of the Russell Byers Charter School,

who brought me joy at a time of great sorrow

by amazing, astounding, and surprising me

in all that they do

There are books out there that will attempt to guide you towards a "perfect life."

This is not one of them.

Look at the warthog. Have you ever seen a more imperfect creature? That's life. That's me. Covered in warts and full of flaws, my path has been anything but pretty. Why hide it? I have experienced a bumpy ride. I have wallowed in the mud at times and sometimes even enjoyed it.

Every day, the warthog encounters the "Big Five" on the savanna — rhinos, lions, elephants, leopards and Cape buffalo. In our daily lives, we struggle with our own "Big Five" — questions of identity, purpose, relationships, crises, and health.

A successful life is a lot like a day on the African plains: sometimes we don't feel safe. Thriving has little to do with who, where, why, what or when things happen to us, and everything to do with how we respond.

This is a book about choice. Our reactions, not our circumstances, create our story.

There's a lot to be learned from the scrappy warthog, who climbs out of its hole to face life head on...

...with tail up!

Here are some of the wonderings and realizations I've had along the way.

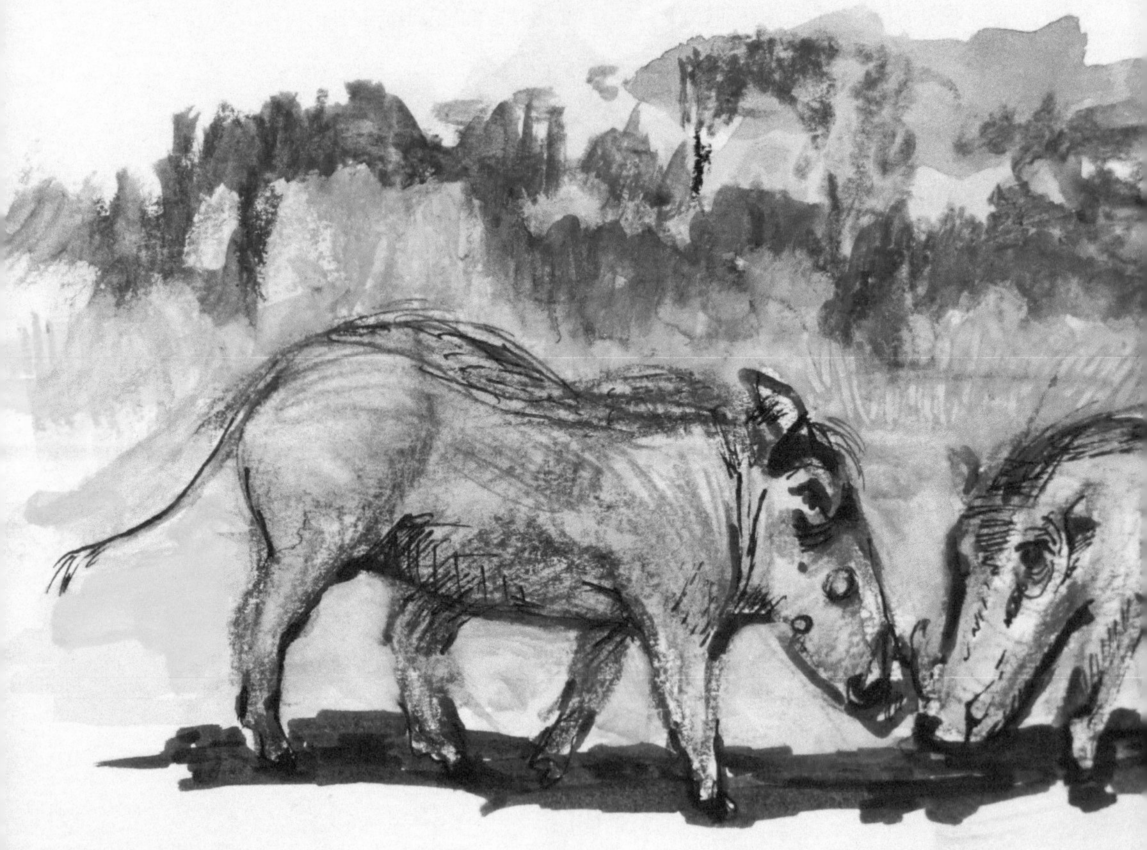

On Identity

Who Defines Me?

When I was six, my grandmother, the original Laurada, told me that I didn't deserve to be her namesake. What's more, she would have preferred that my prettier, smarter, nicer sister had been named Laurada instead.

How painful!

That conversation was stinging and unforgettable. It took years of healing and growing before I finally became determined not to allow the words of others to shape my identity.

Only I can decide what it means to be Laurada.

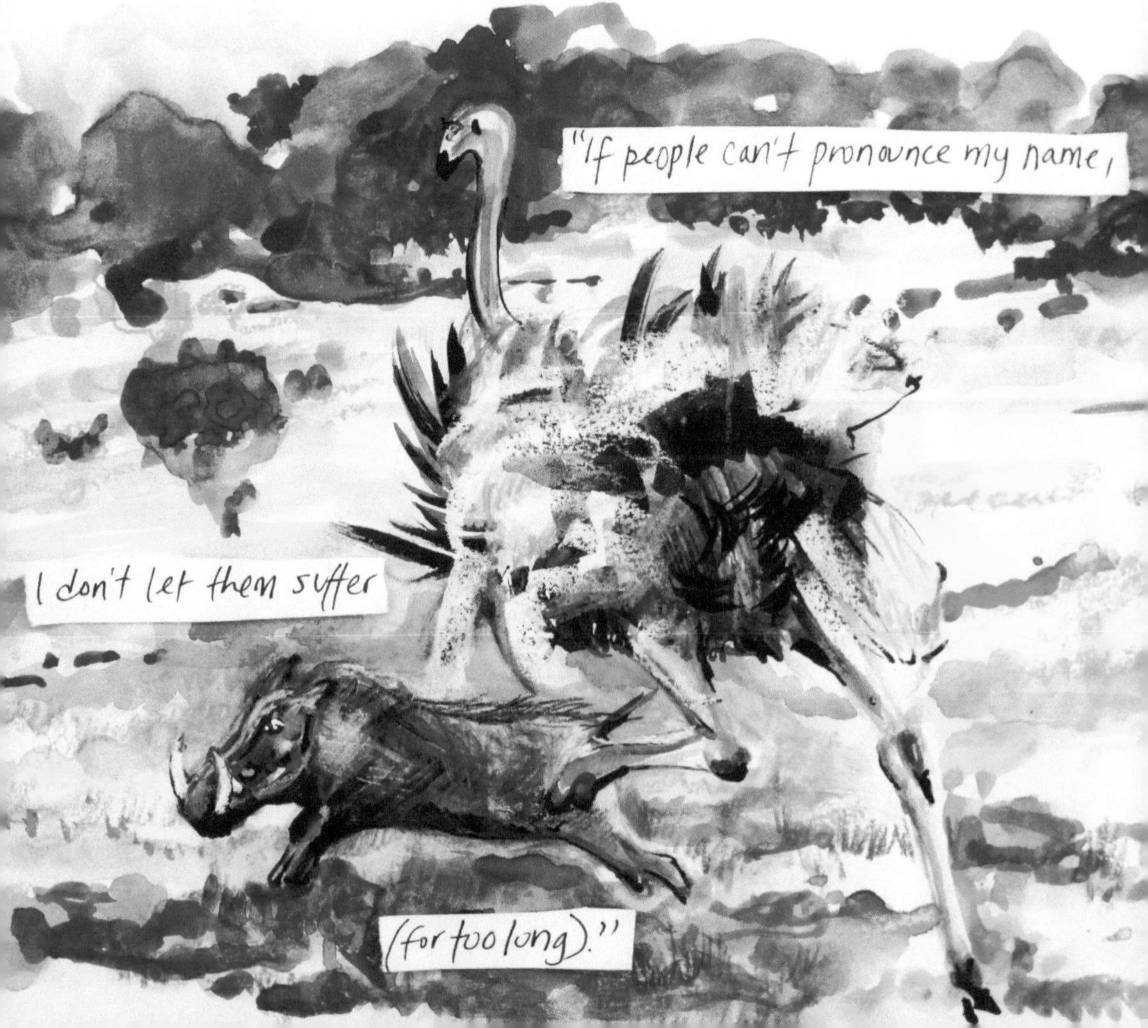
"If people can't pronounce my name,
I don't let them suffer
(for too long)."

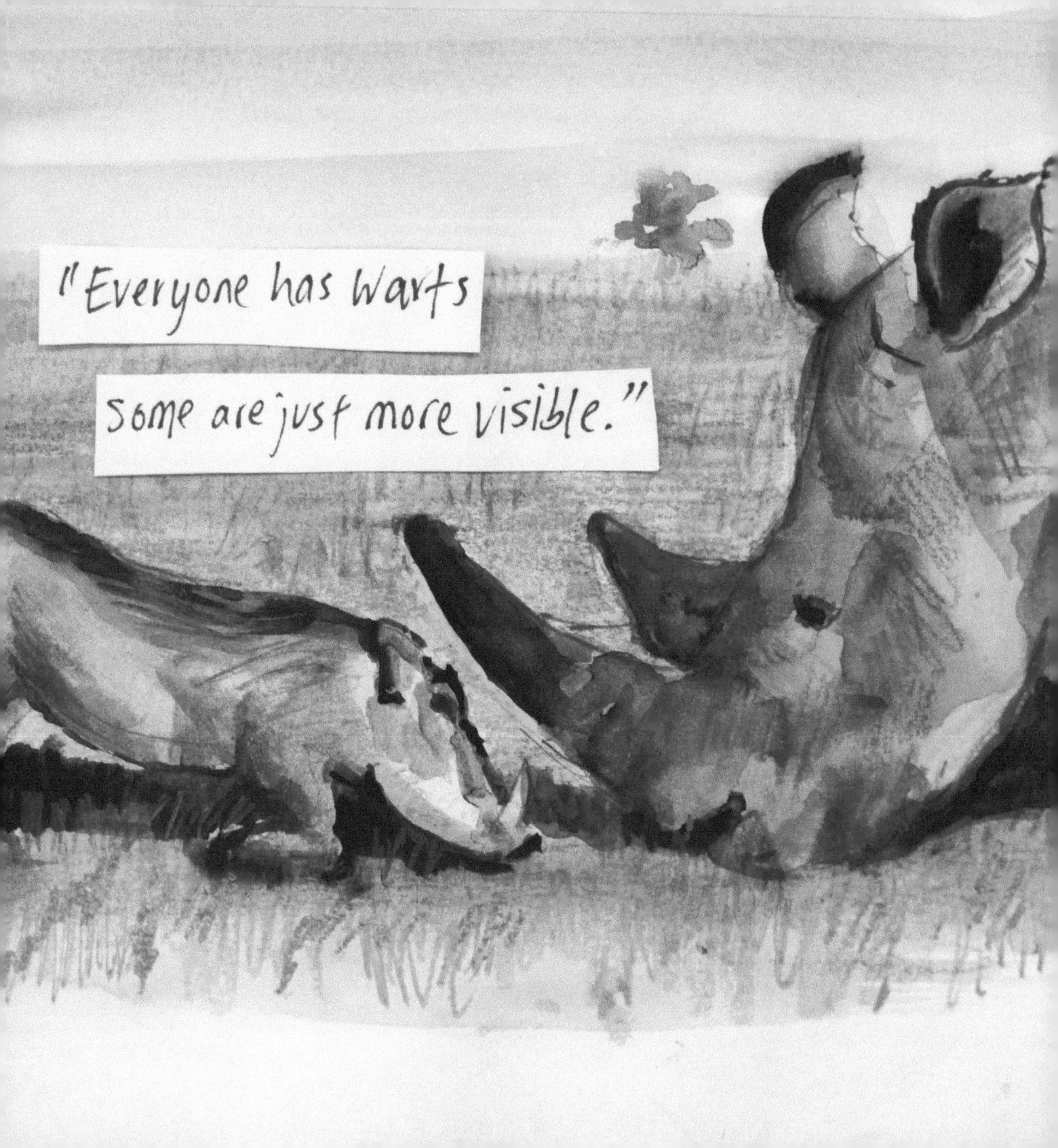
"Everyone has warts
some are just more visible."

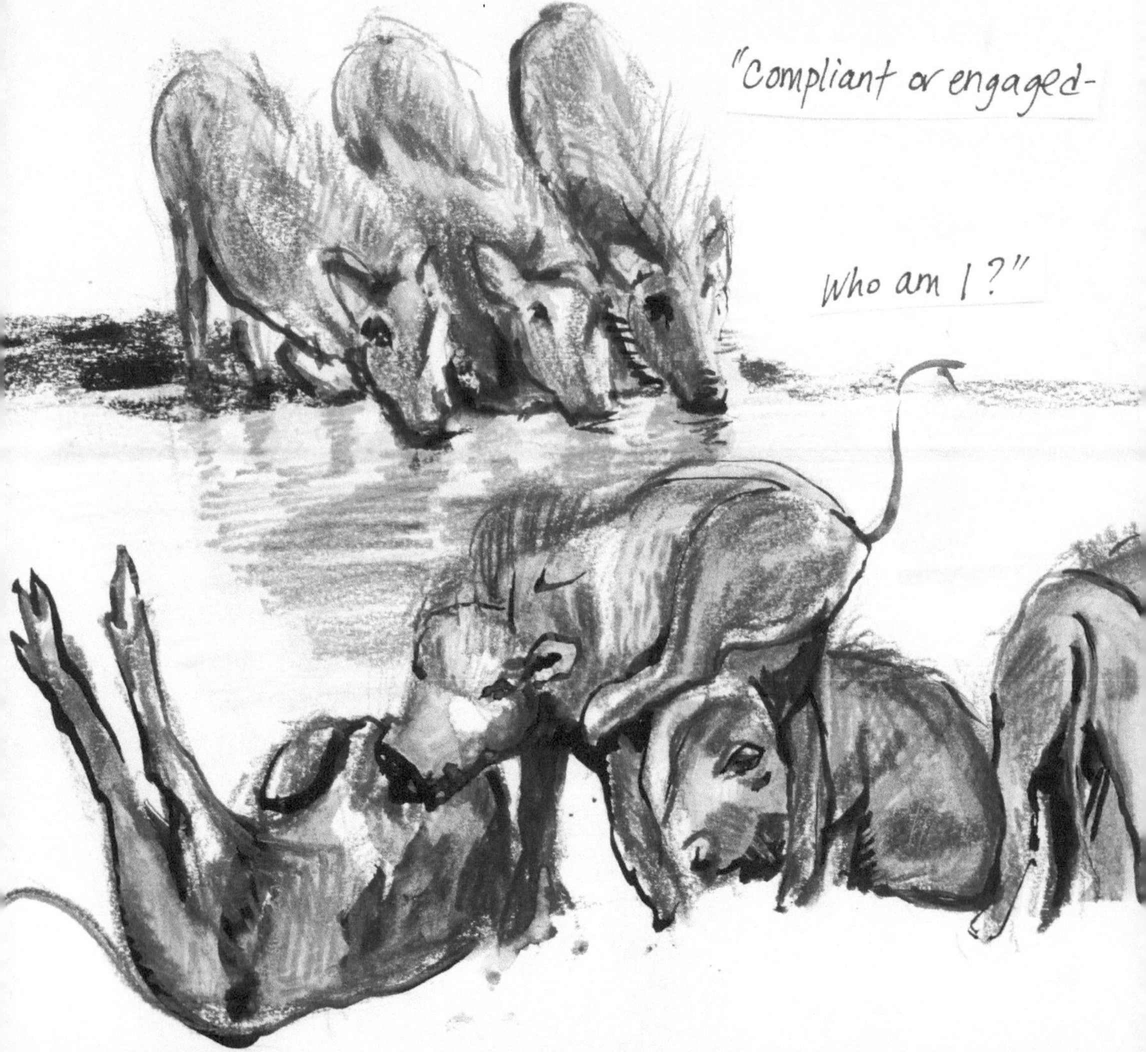
"Compliant or engaged-
Who am I?"

"Only I can be responsible for my life."

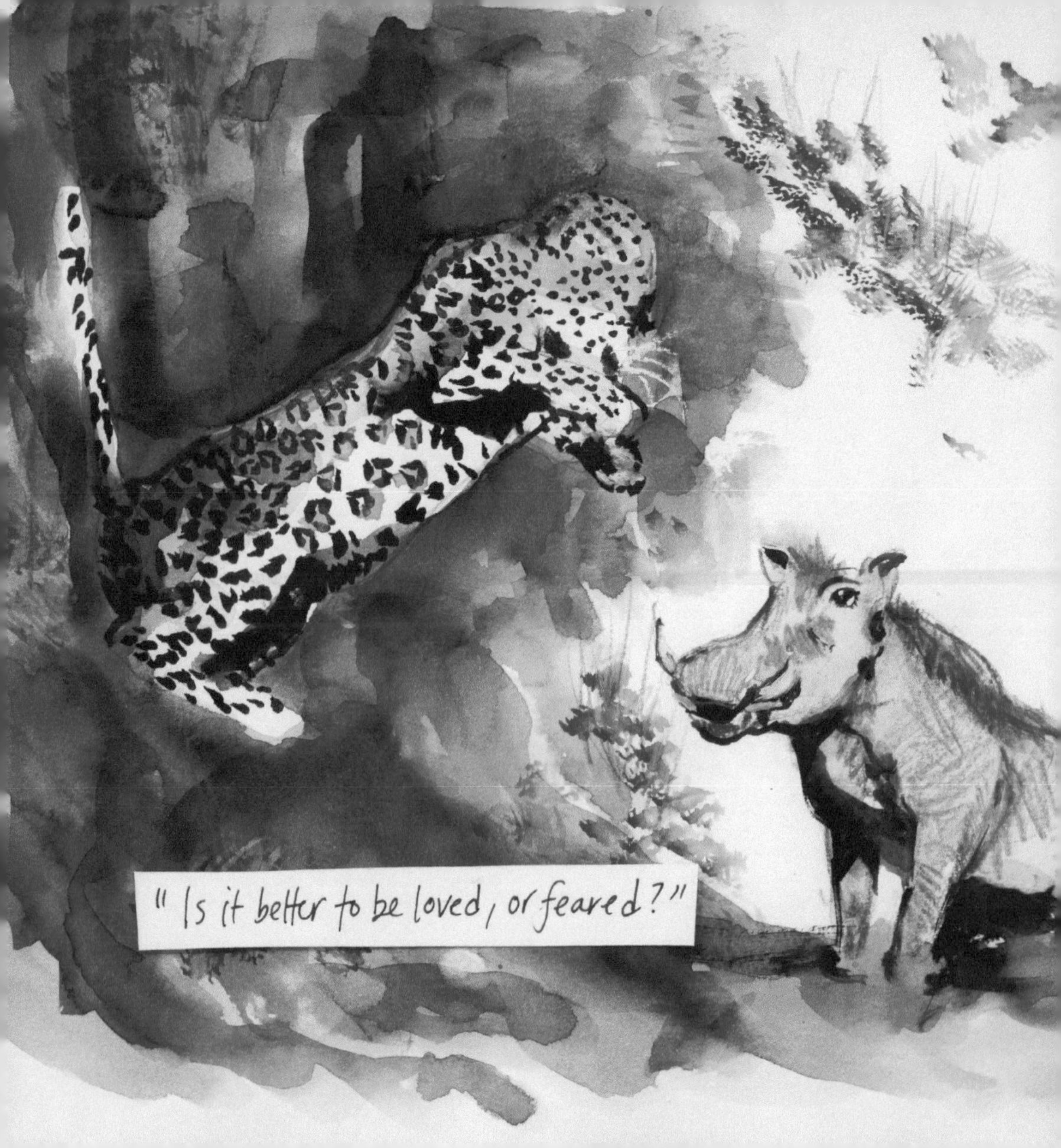
"Is it better to be loved, or feared?"

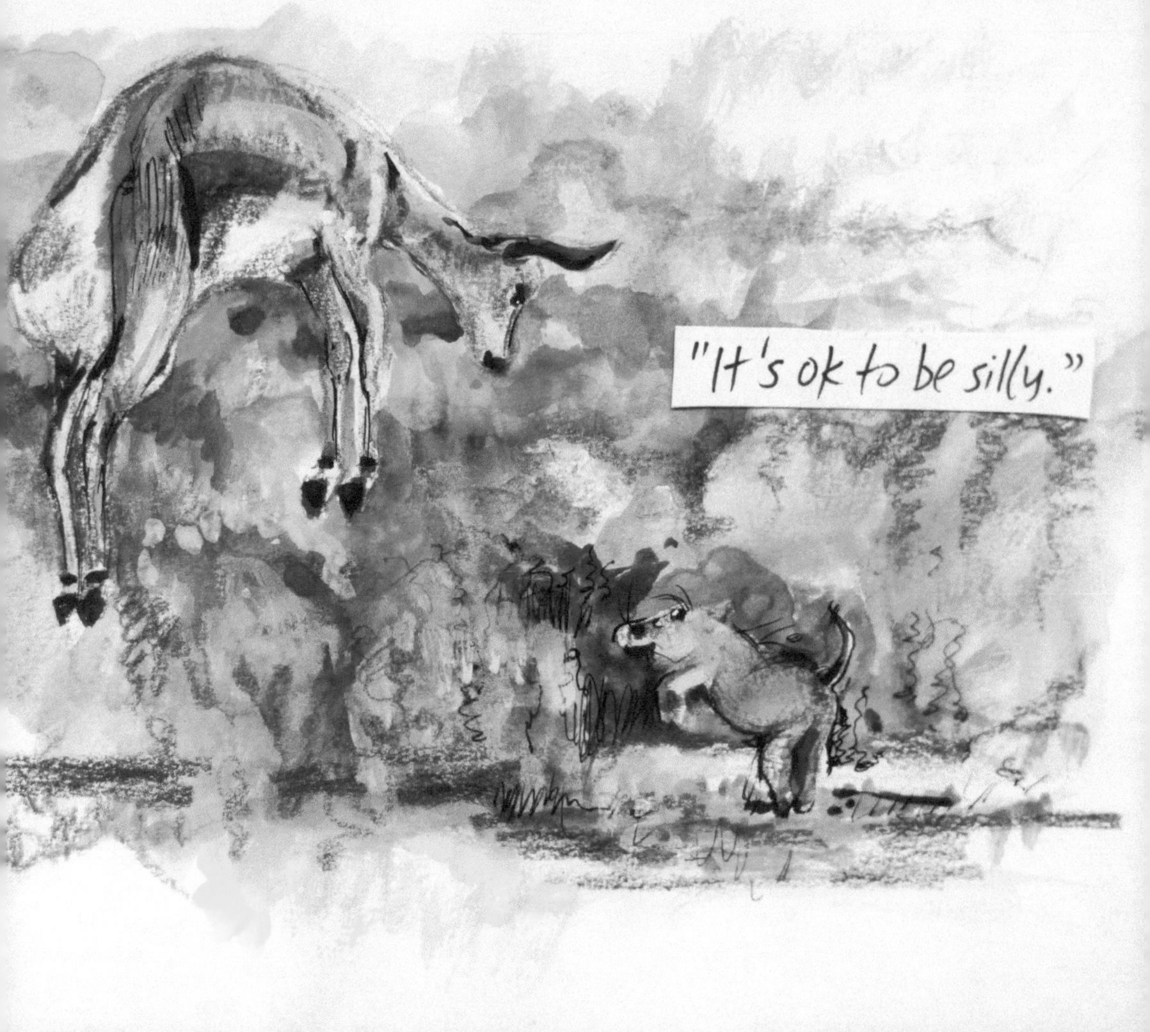
"It's ok to be silly."

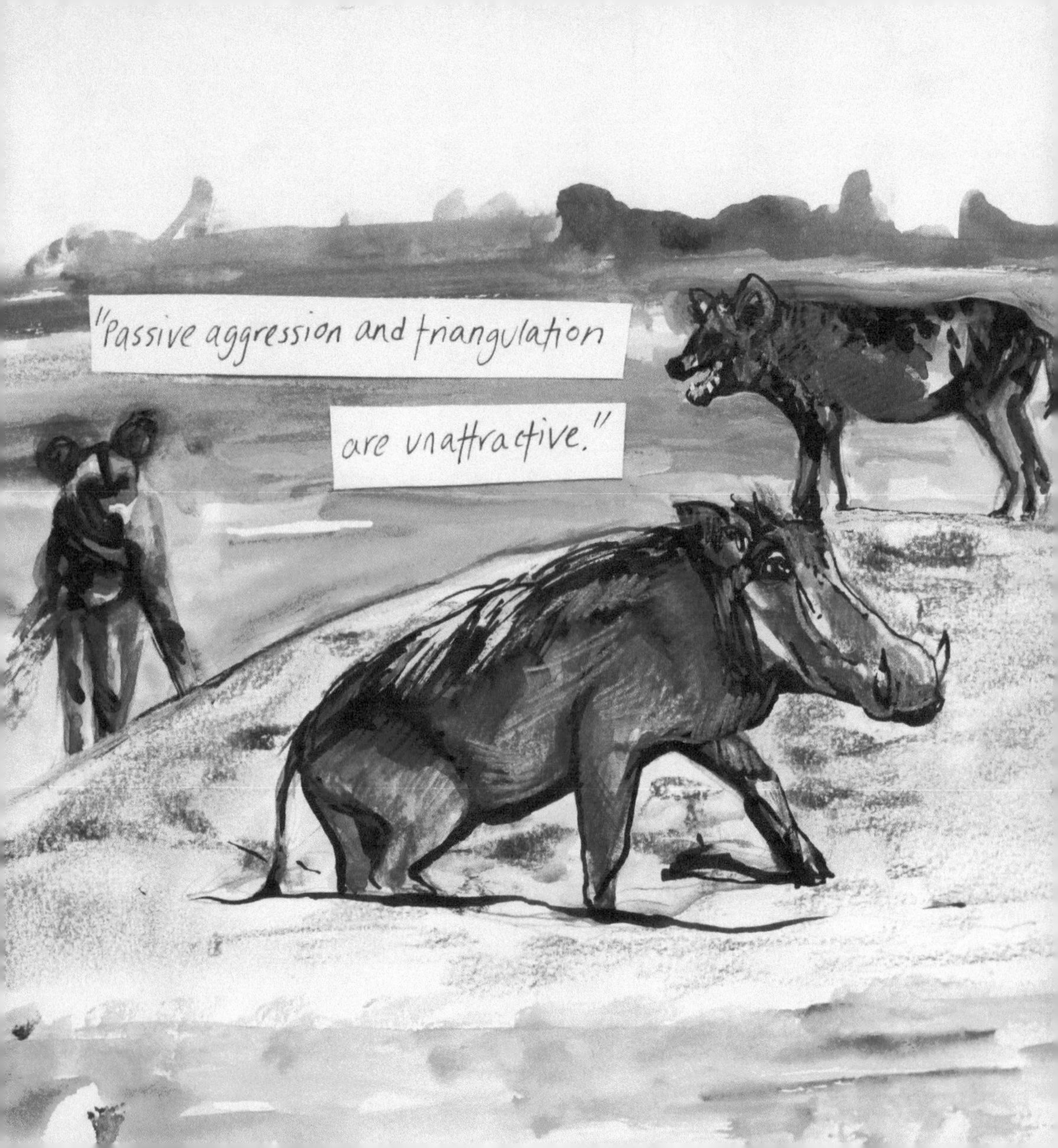
"Passive aggression and triangulation
are unattractive."

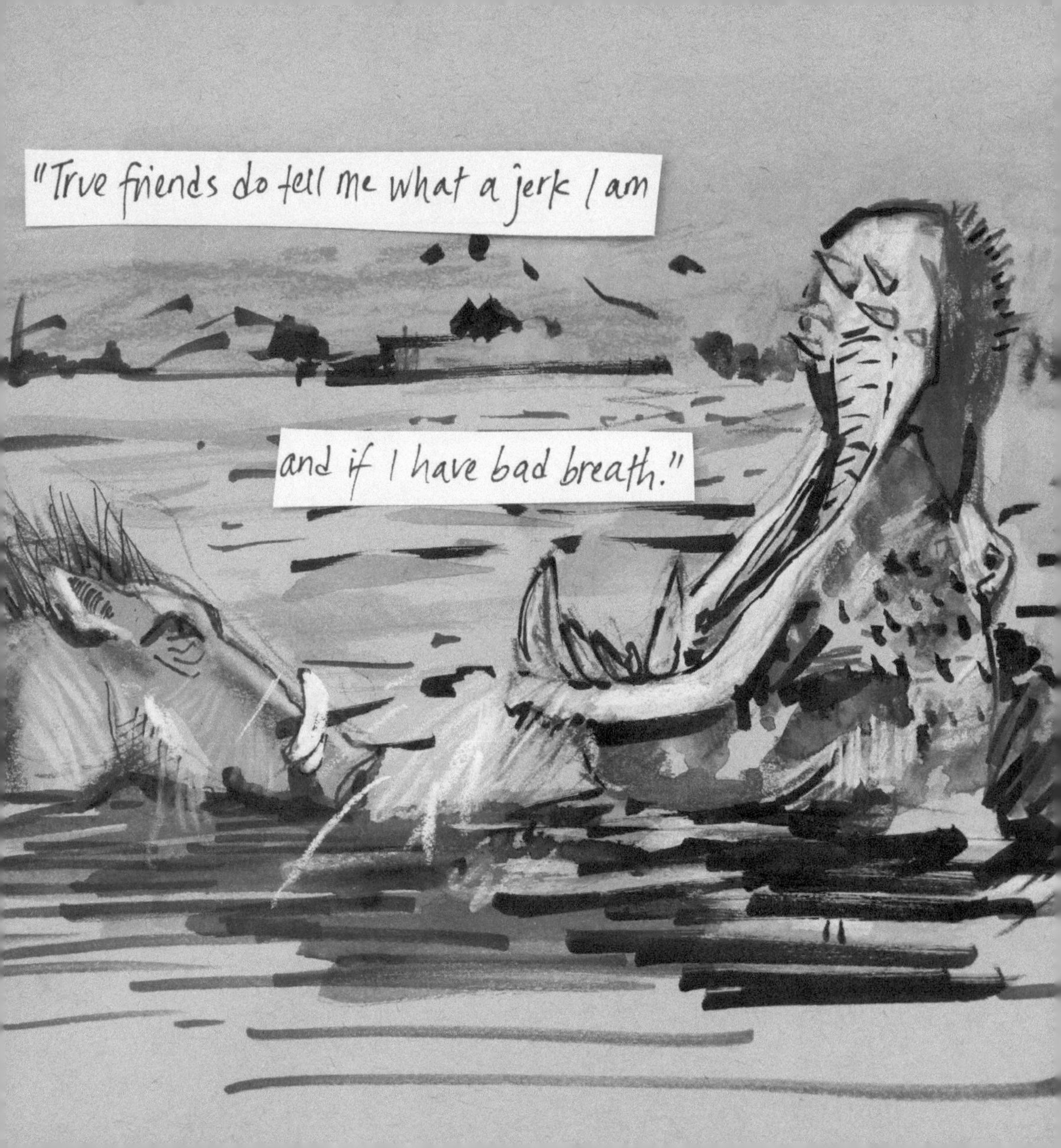
"True friends do tell me what a jerk I am
and if I have bad breath."

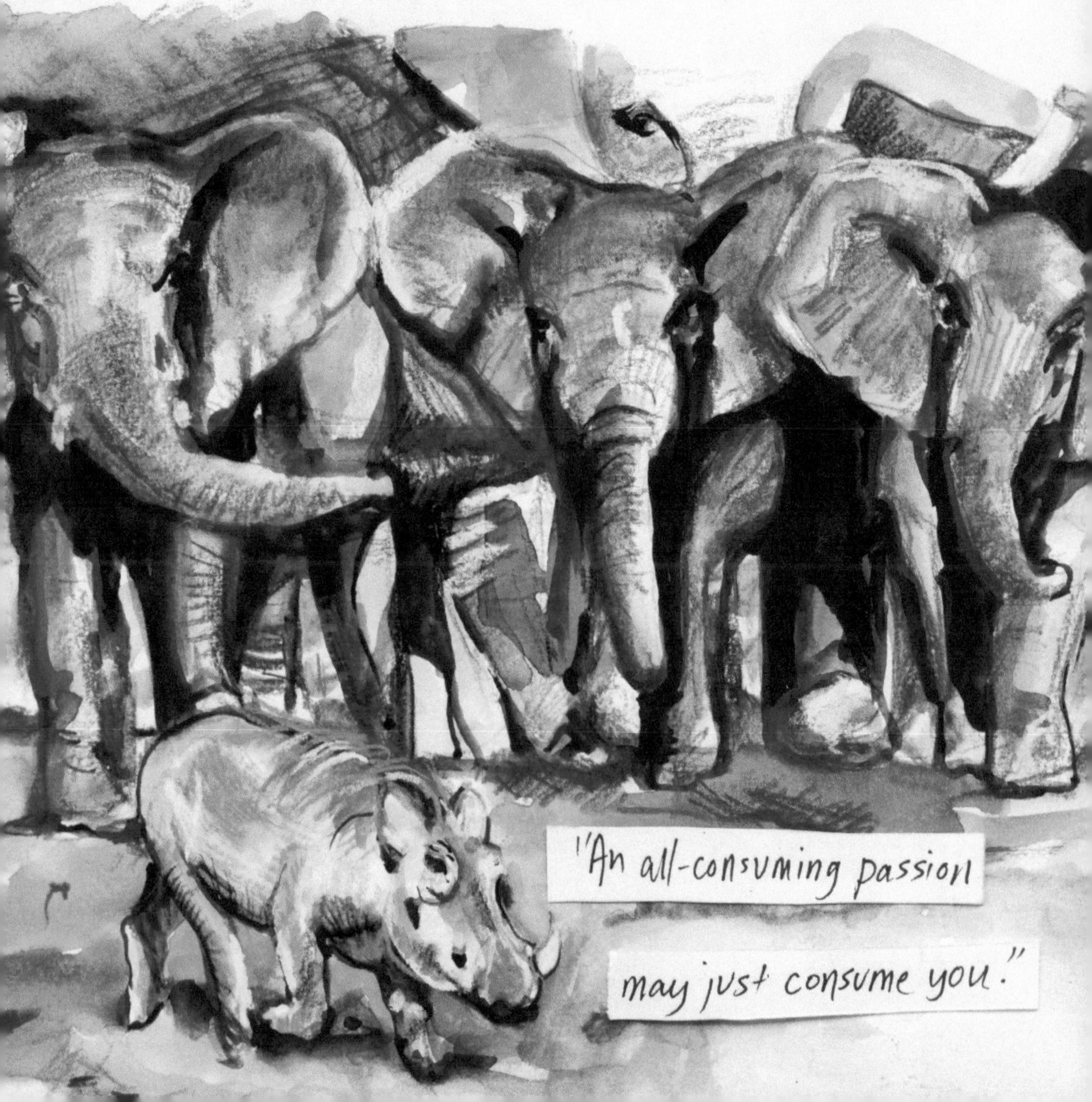
"An all-consuming passion
may just consume you."

"I only swear when people least expect it."

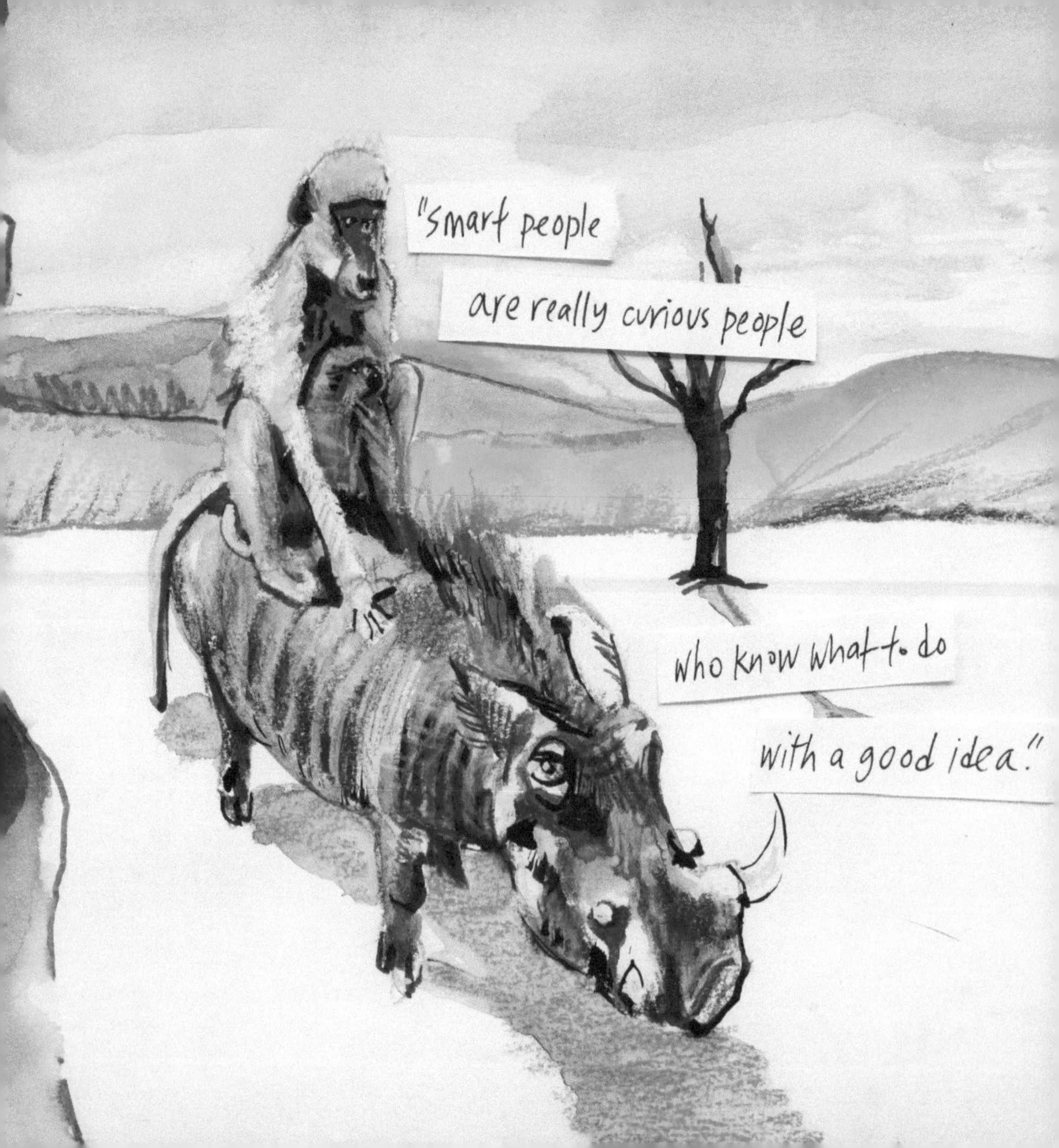
"Smart people
are really curious people
who know what to do
with a good idea."

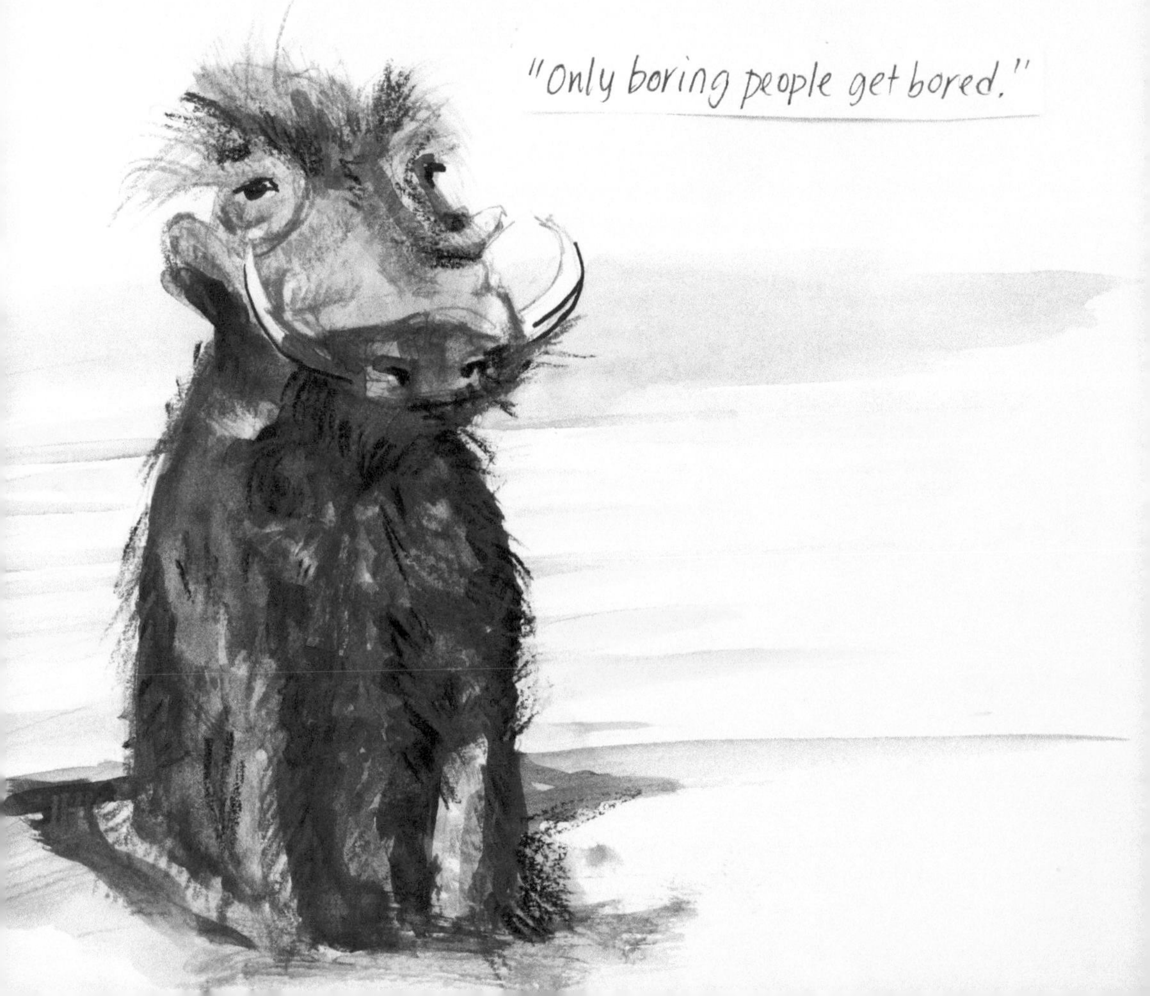
"Only boring people get bored."

On Purpose

Where To Begin?

My 40th birthday present to myself was to get an MBA.

There was only one problem — I didn't get in.

The day I received my rejection letter, I walked into the admissions office and assured them I would be attending their program — the only question was how. I left the office with a list of classes to complete at the school's undergraduate college and was told that the minimum requirement was straight A's. Many front row seats and countless hand-raises later, I got in.

Don't ask yourself if you will achieve your goals. Find out how you're going to achieve them.

—Laurada Byers, MBA

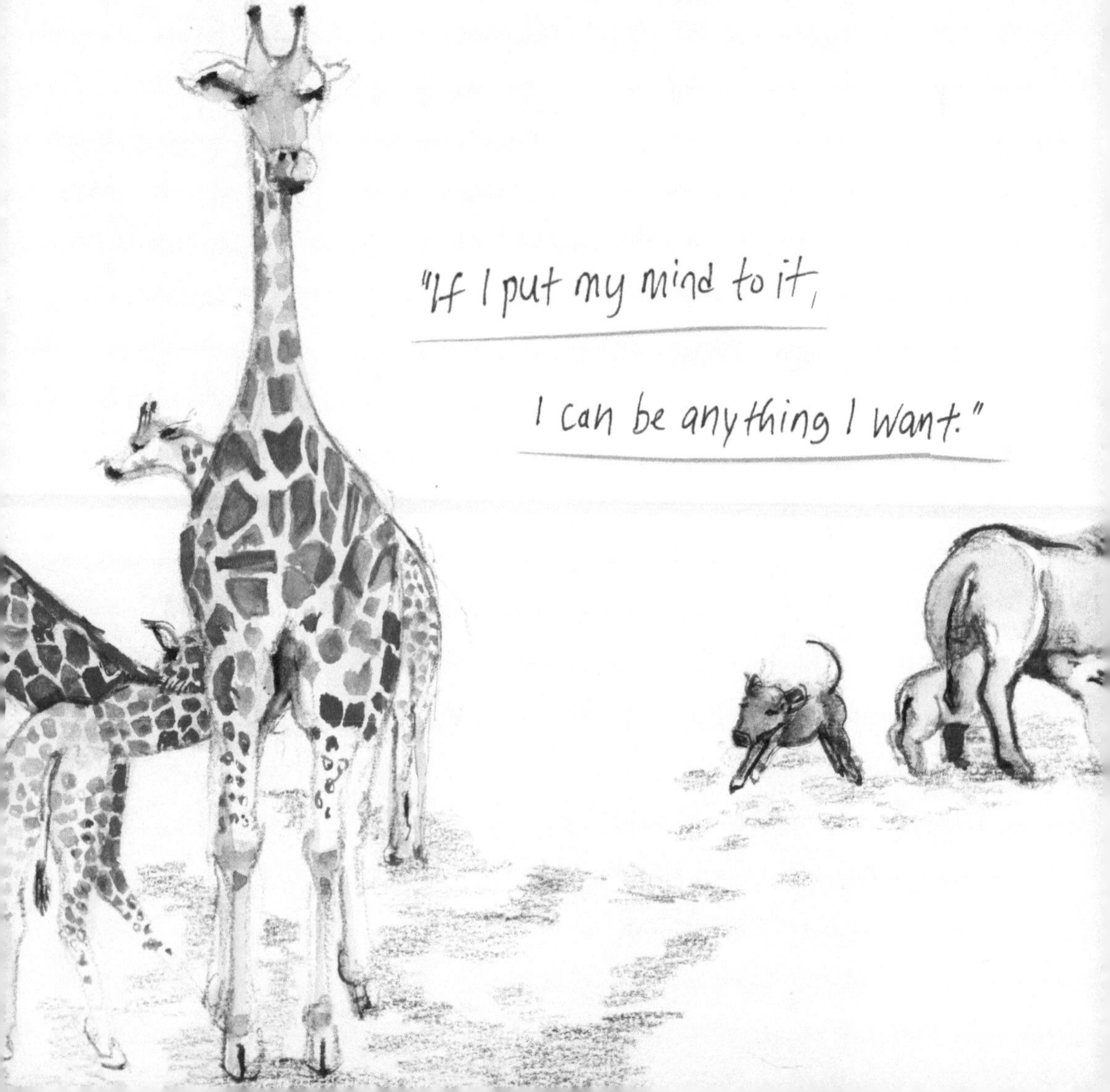

"If I put my mind to it,

I can be anything I want."

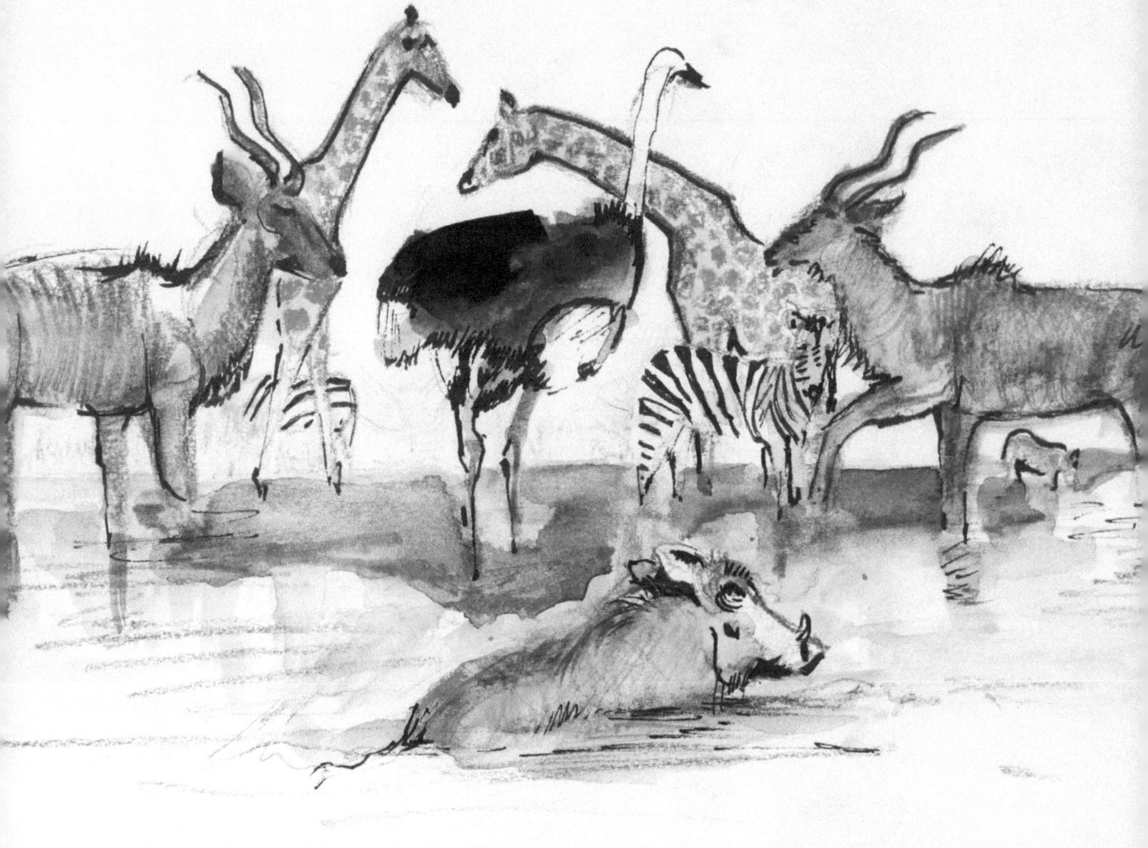

"Too many choices make me cry."

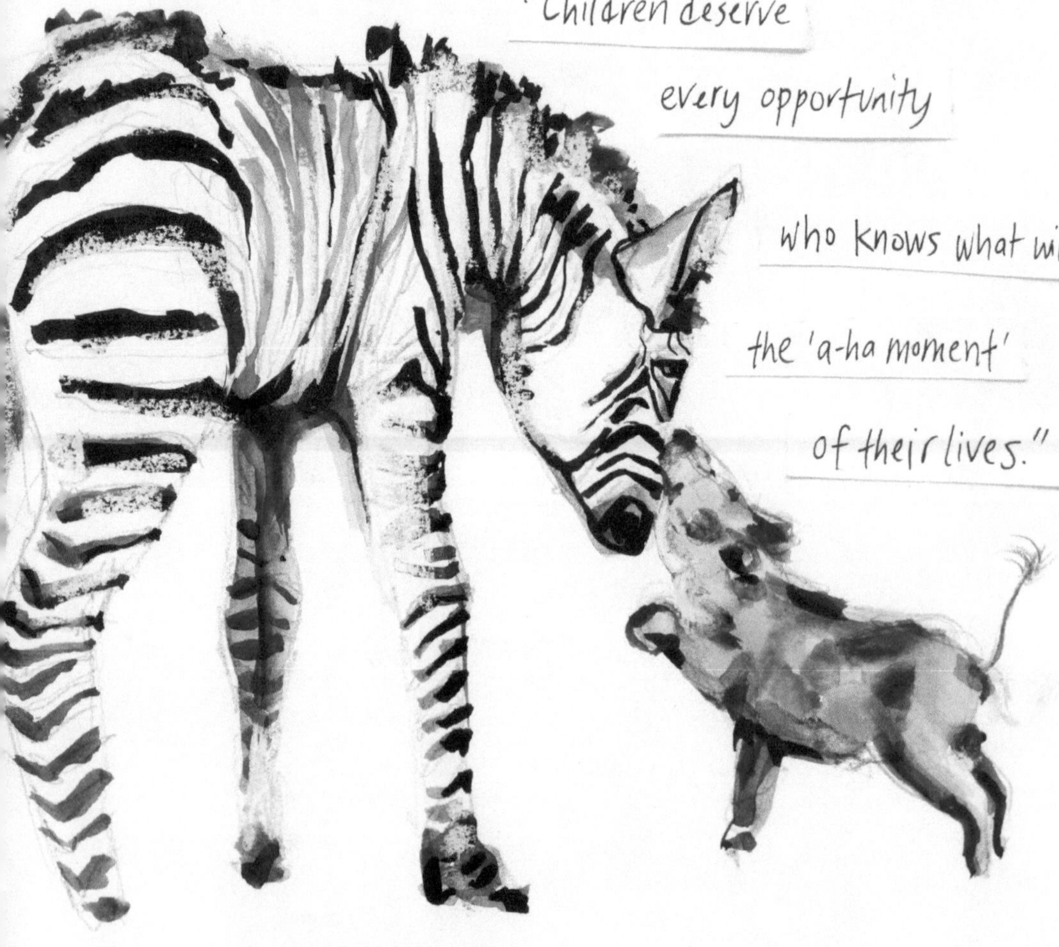

"Children deserve
every opportunity
who knows what will be
the 'a-ha moment'
of their lives."

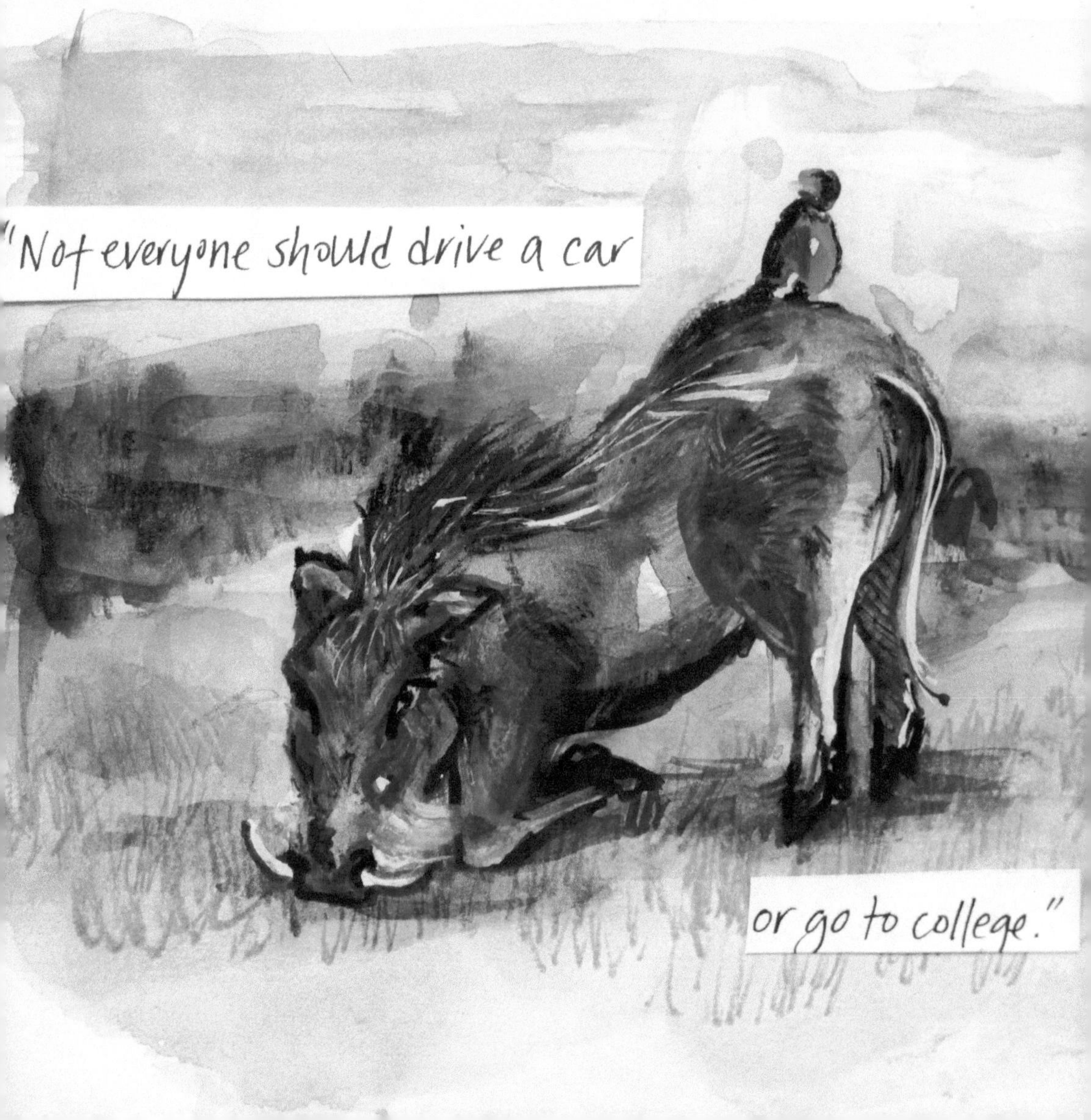
"Not everyone should drive a car
or go to college."

"There are no wrong answers."

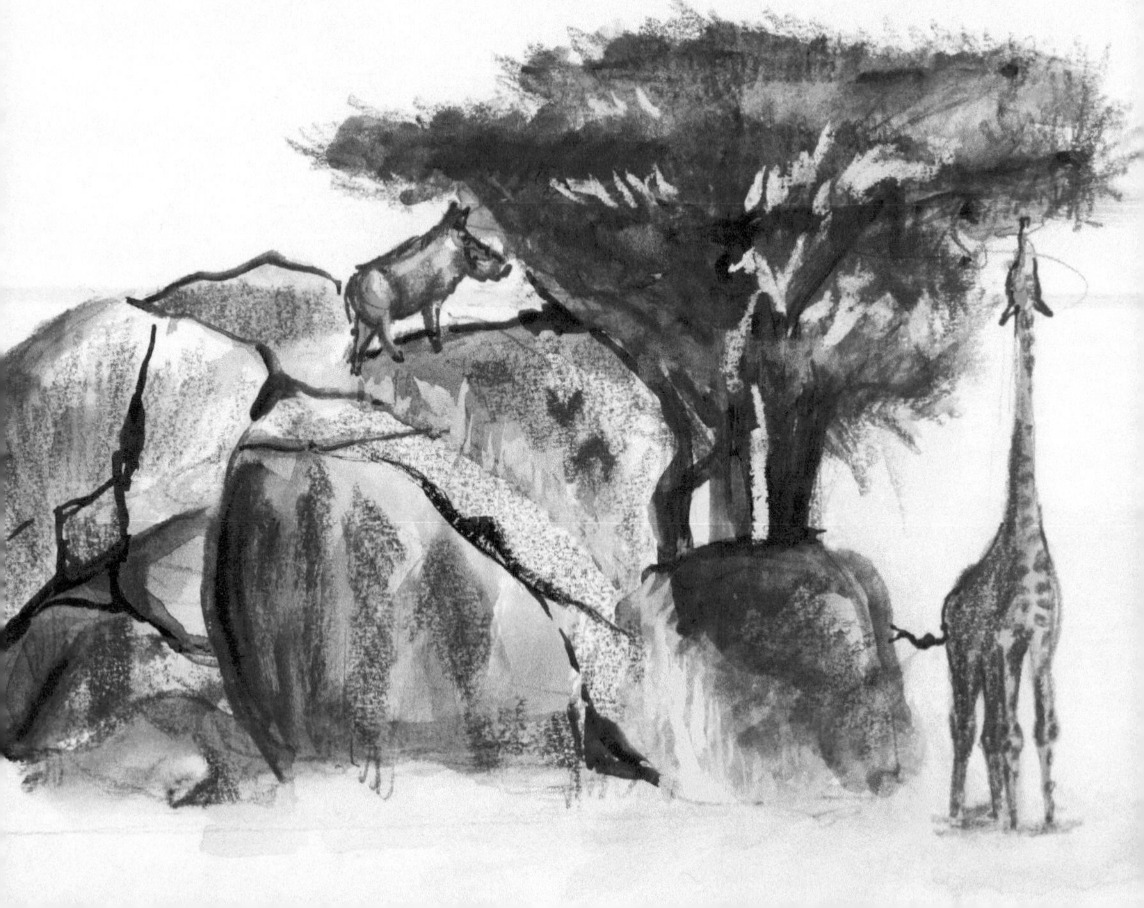

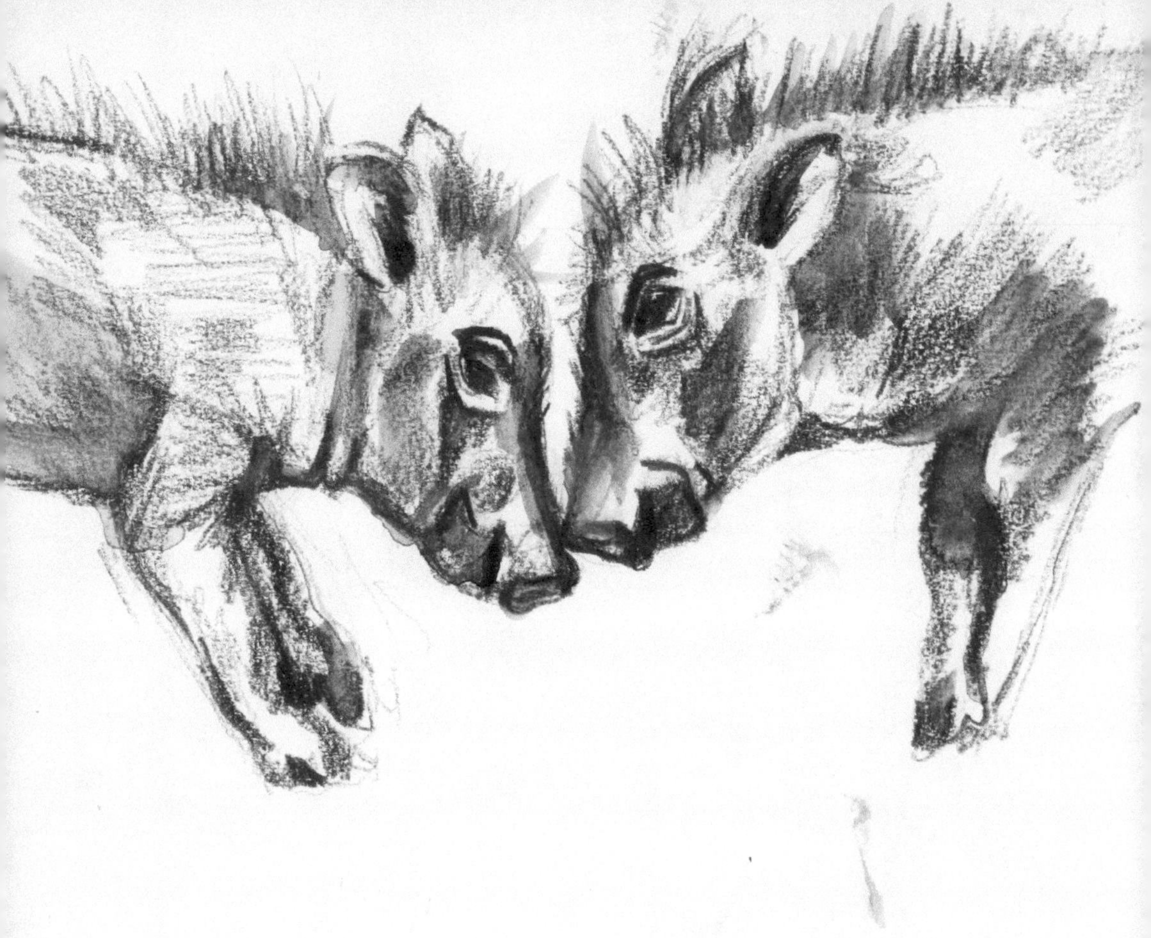

"Success and failure are twins."

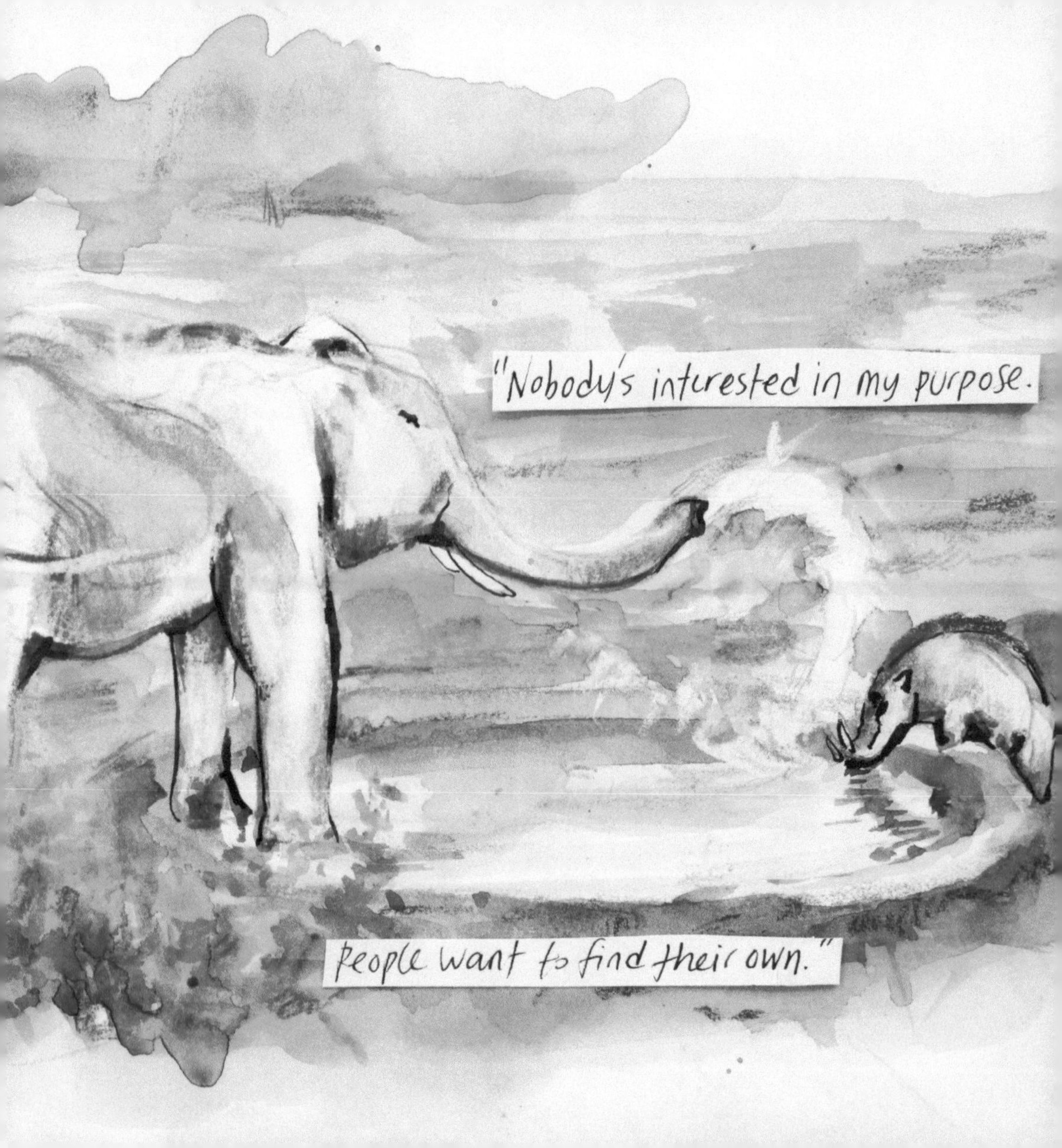
"Nobody's interested in my purpose.
People want to find their own."

"Fake it 'til you make it."

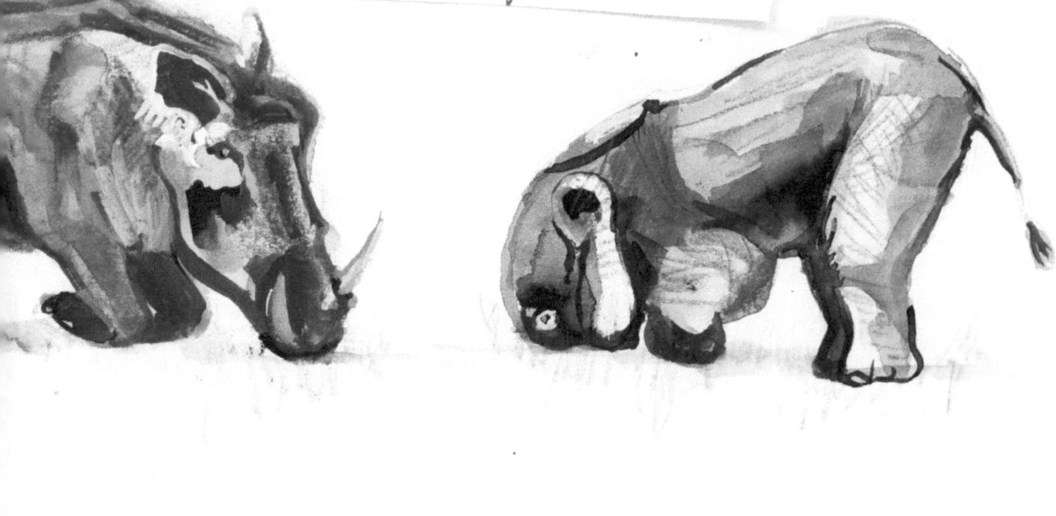

"Maintaining the status quo really means I'm going backwards."

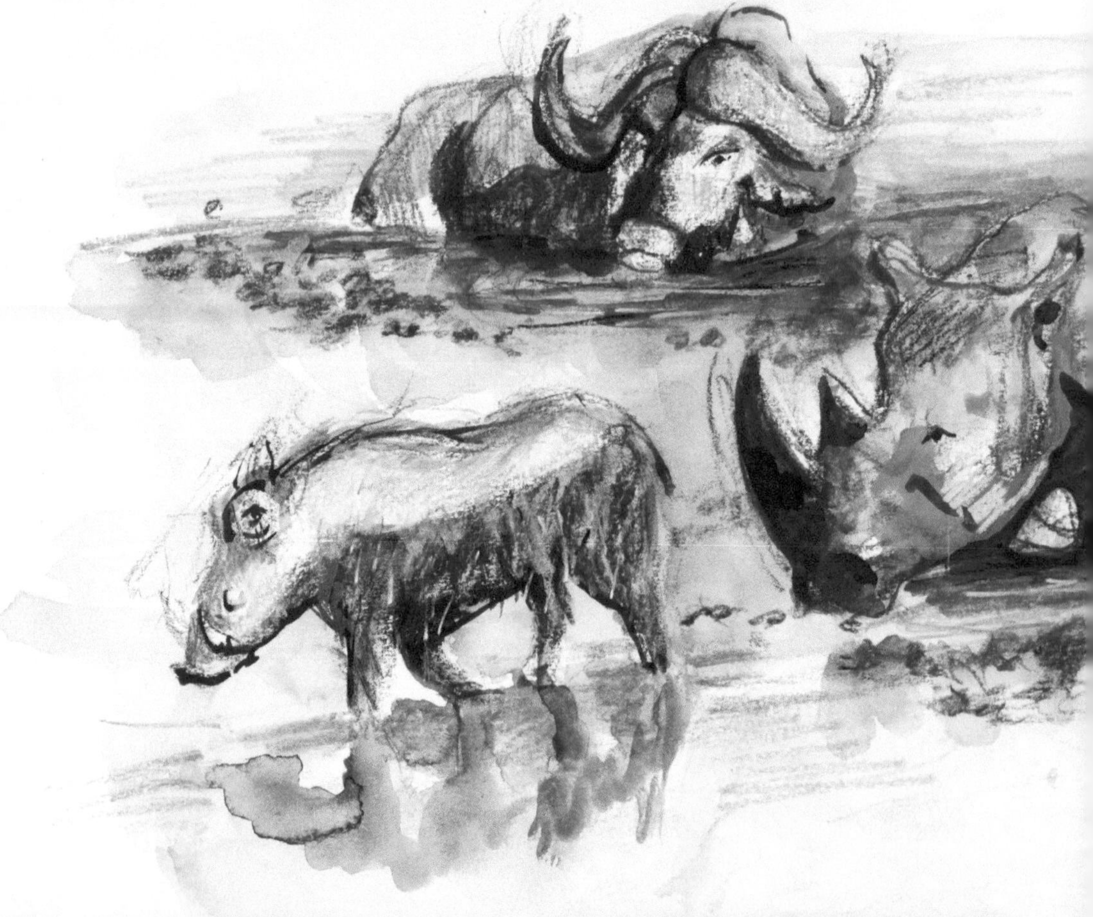

"Attitude is everything."

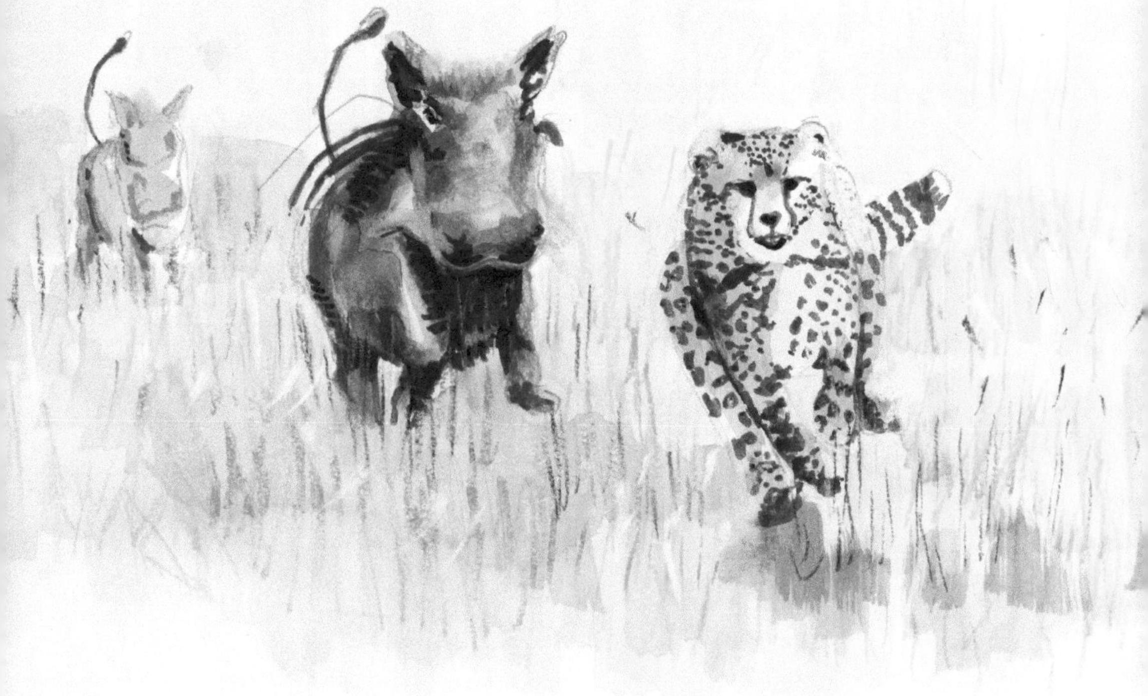

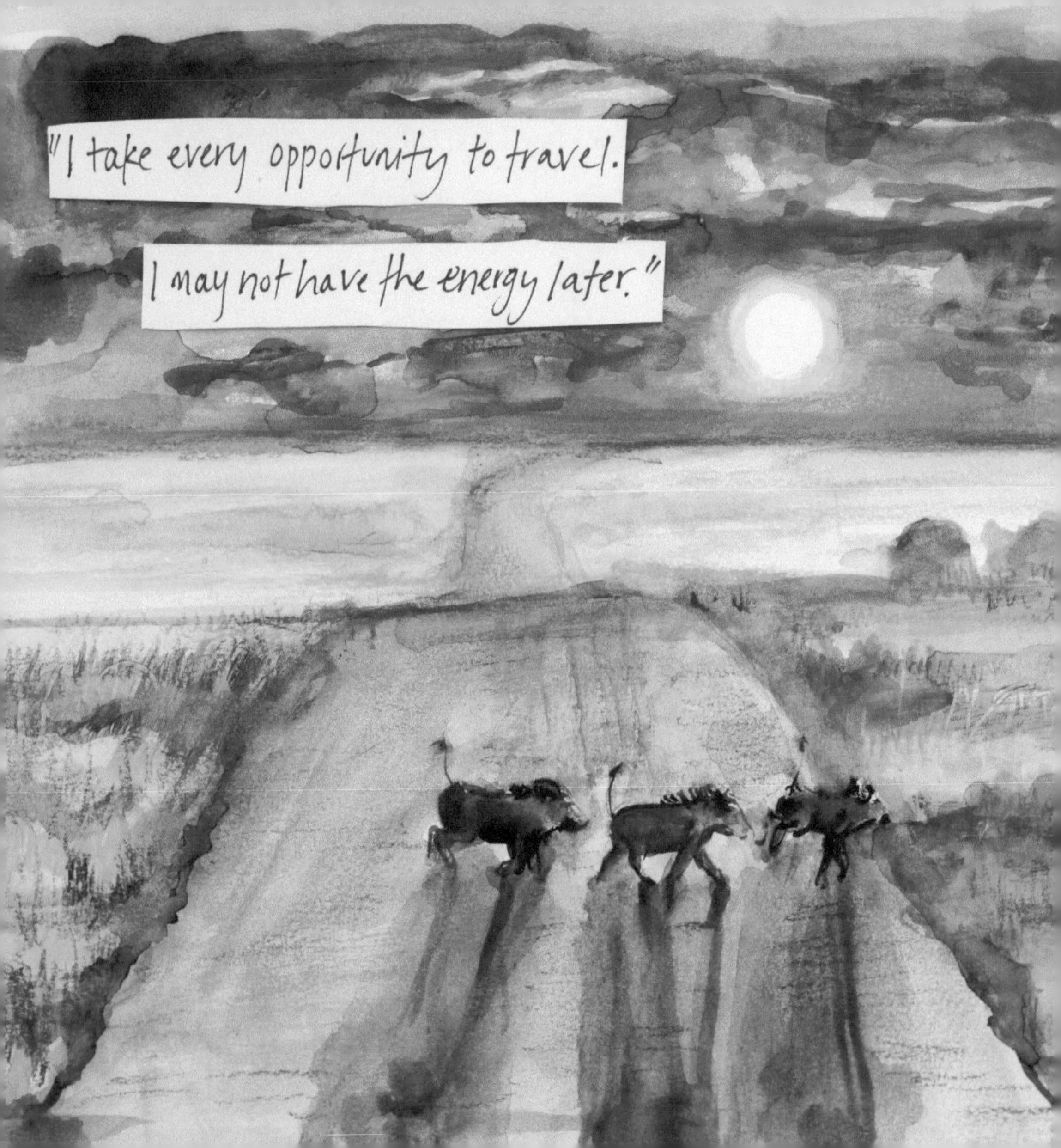
"I take every opportunity to travel.
I may not have the energy later."

"It's hard to hitchhike without a map."

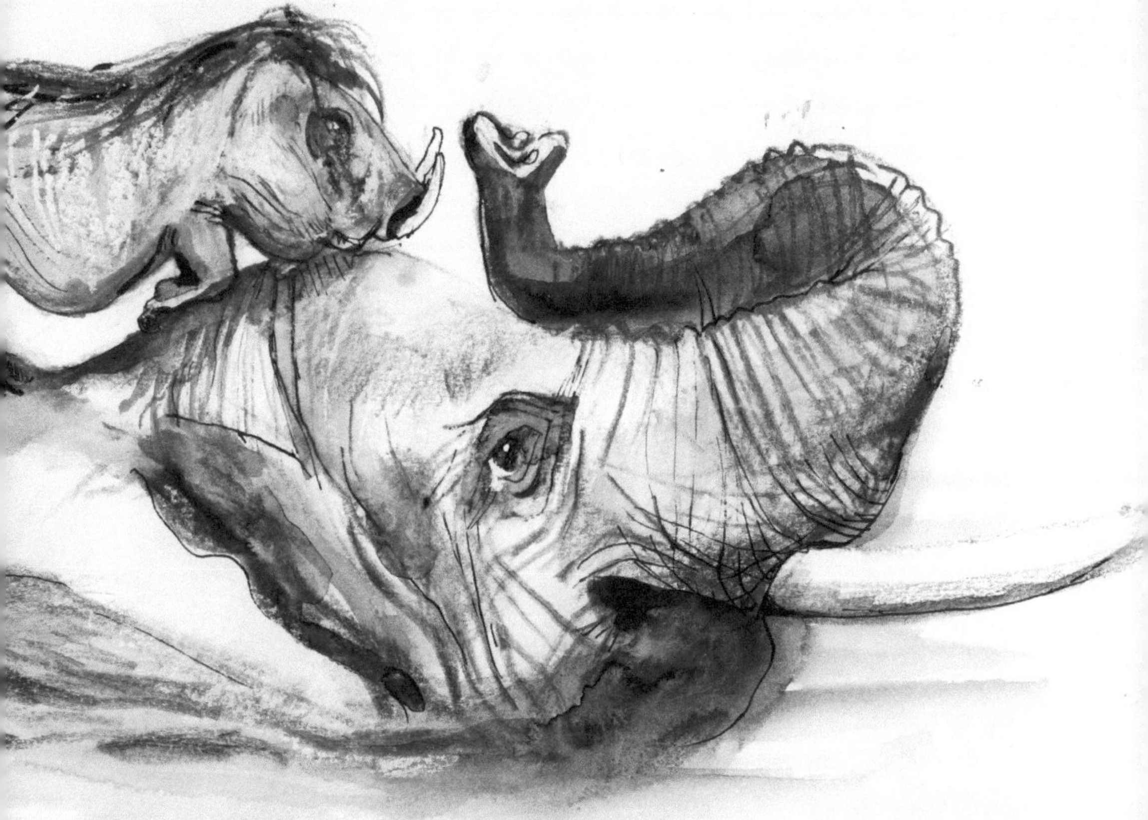

On Relationships

Why Love Endures?

When I married the love of my life, Russell Byers, in 1972, life was good- exciting and full of surprises. How lucky we were. It all changed in an instant.

While driving home from a dinner party in December 1999, Russell and I stopped to buy ice cream near our home. The time between choosing chocolate or vanilla and a teenager pulling a knife in the parking lot has become a silent blur. As the young man approached us, Russell steered him further into the shadows, away from me, as I backed toward the fluorescent lights of the convenience store.

Was I screaming when my husband fell violently through the glass doors of the store into a pool of his own blood? Kneeling on the cold, white, linoleum floor, I was numb to the police pleading "Ma'am! Ma'am! Why are you doing CPR? He's dead."

In the weeks following Russell's murder, I couldn't stop feeling overwhelmed by grief and kept reliving the horror of that moment. My refuge was the comfort of my bed. While it was tempting to pull up the covers and sink quietly into the darkness, I suddenly realized that I didn't want the murder of my husband to be the defining moment of my life. Instead, I began to focus on what Russell would have asked: If this nineteen-year-old had been given an equal chance in life, could things have turned out differently?

Yes! Inspired by Russell's love of learning and his belief in the power of education, creating a school in his memory began to take shape. I moved through my pain by facing it head on- I even went to prison to meet the man who killed him. The seed of the Russell Byers Charter School had been planted...

Grief can silence you or give you a voice. It's your choice. Make it a good one.

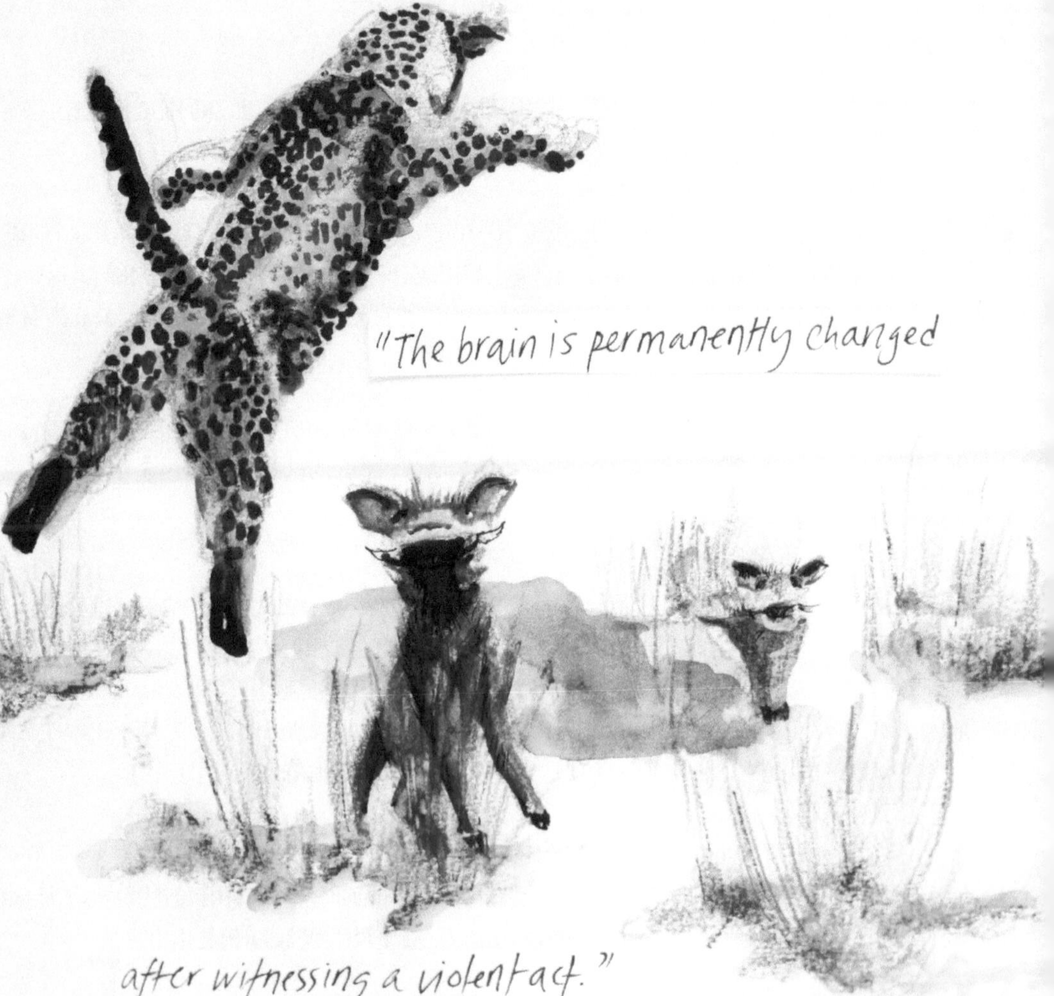

"The brain is permanently changed

after witnessing a violent act."

"Trying to grieve is like being constipated –

you're all scrunched up inside yourself."

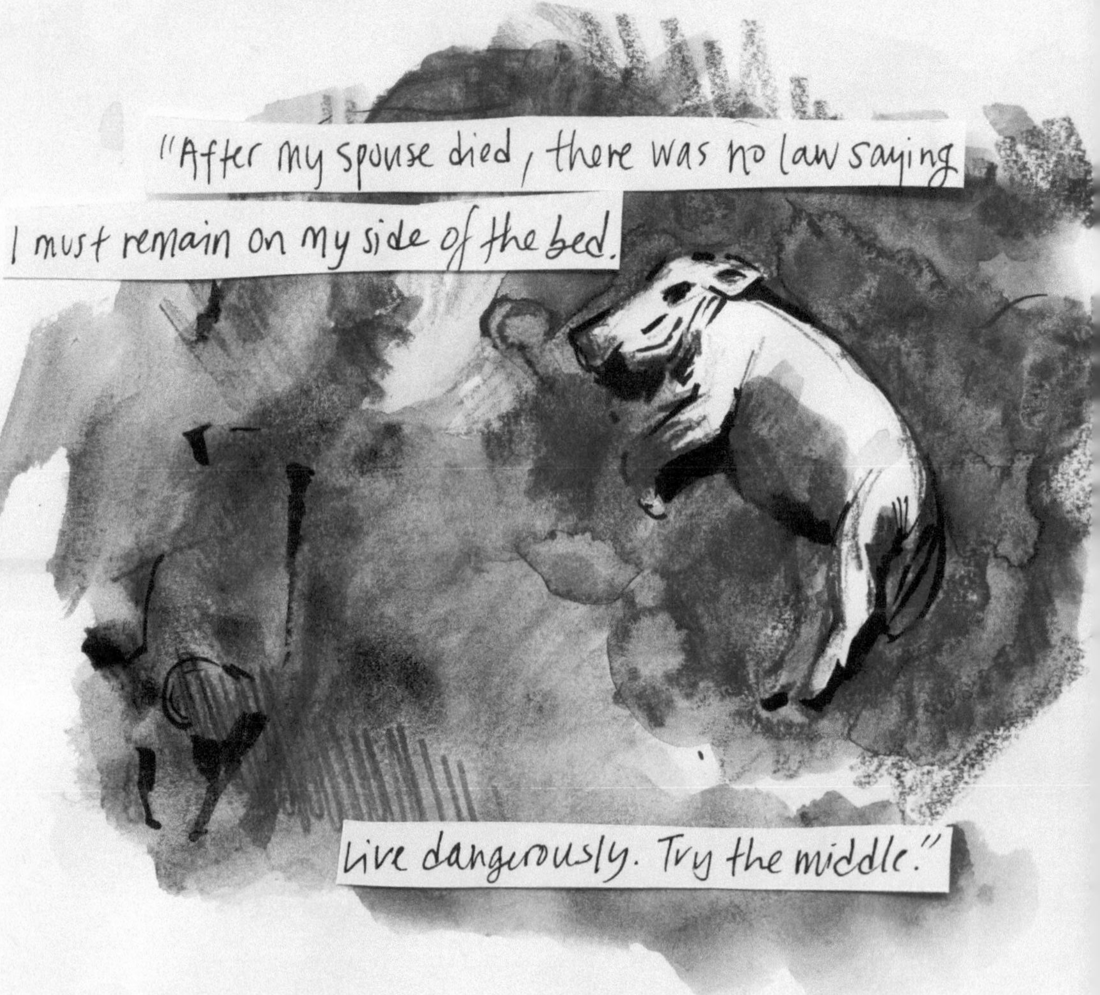
"After my spouse died, there was no law saying
I must remain on my side of the bed.
Live dangerously. Try the middle."

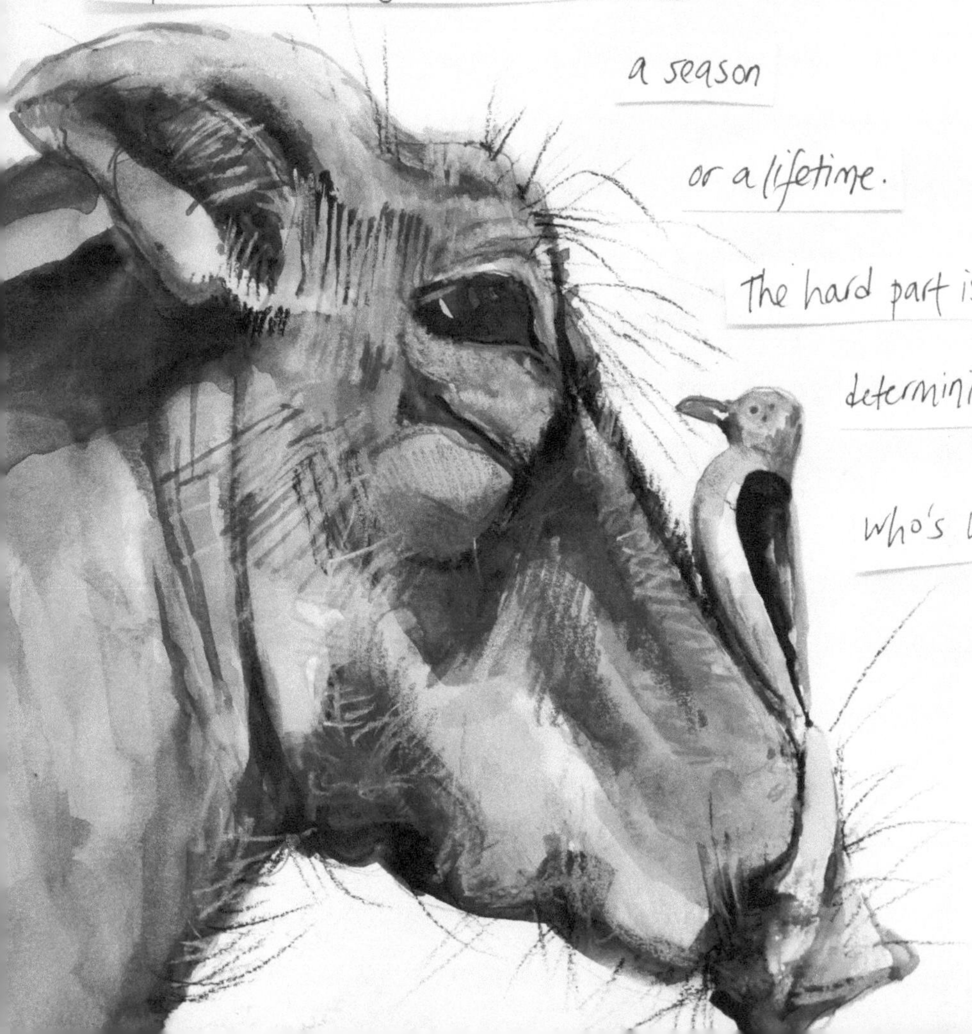

"People come into my life for a reason

a season

or a lifetime.

The hard part is

determining

who's who."

"To snuggle bunny is a verb."

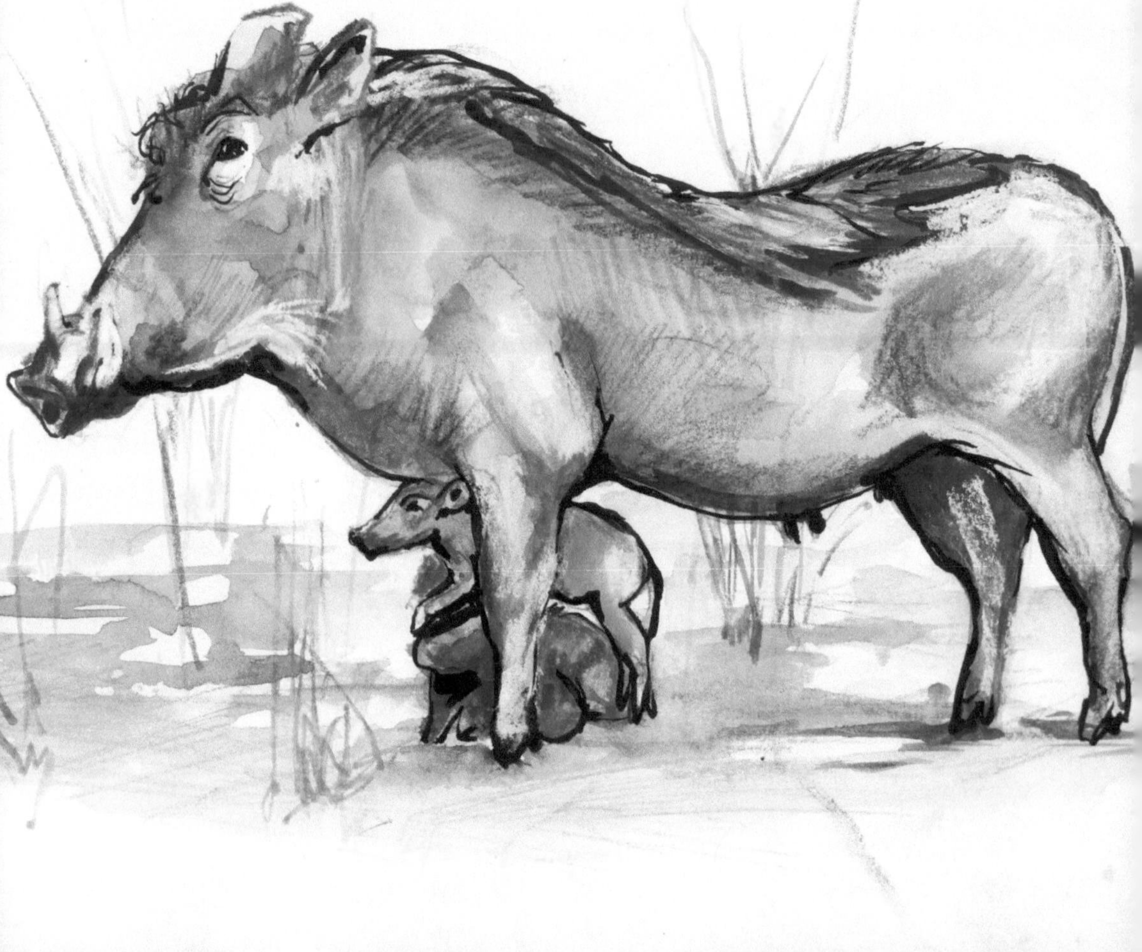

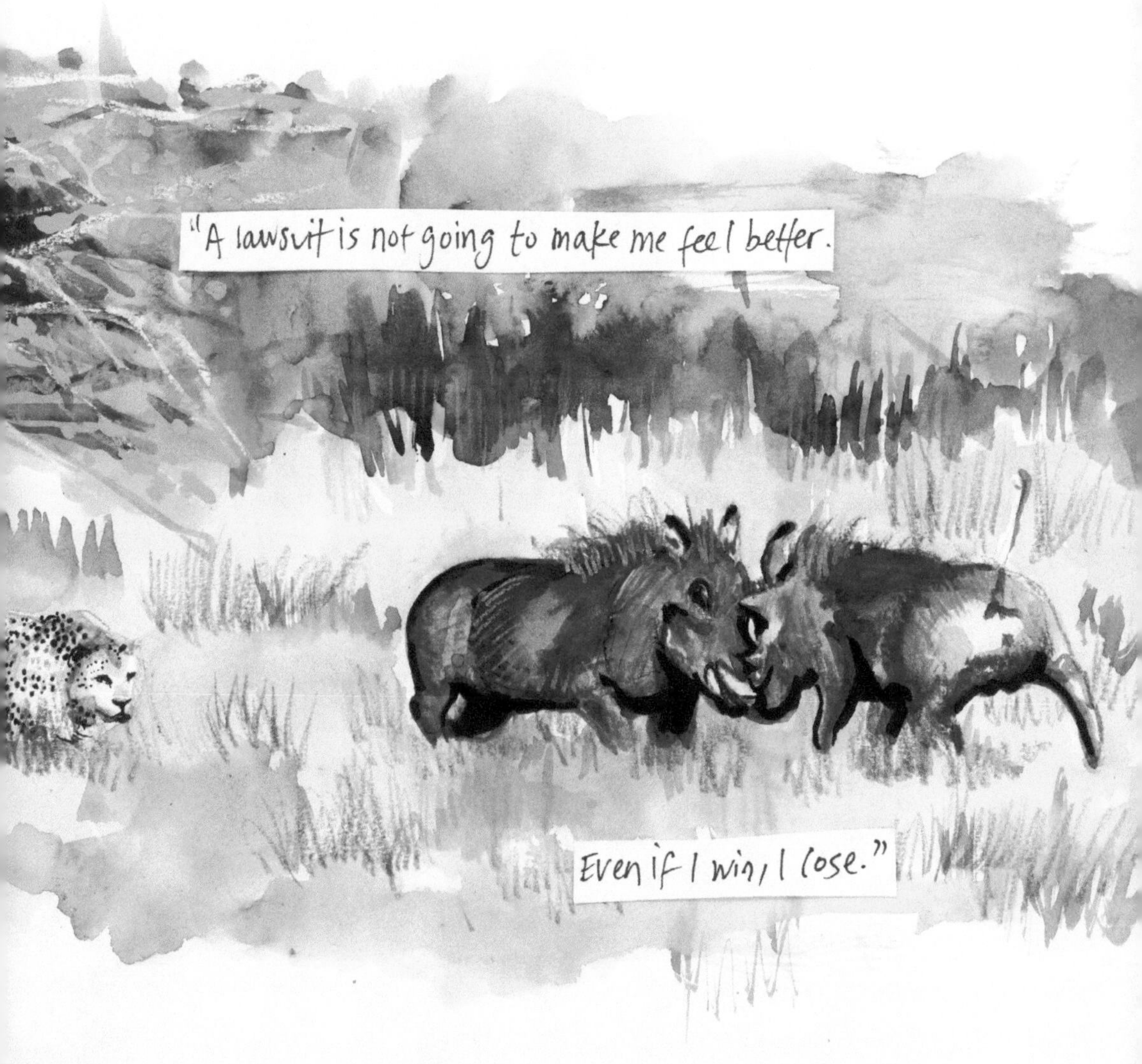
"A lawsuit is not going to make me feel better.
Even if I win, I lose."

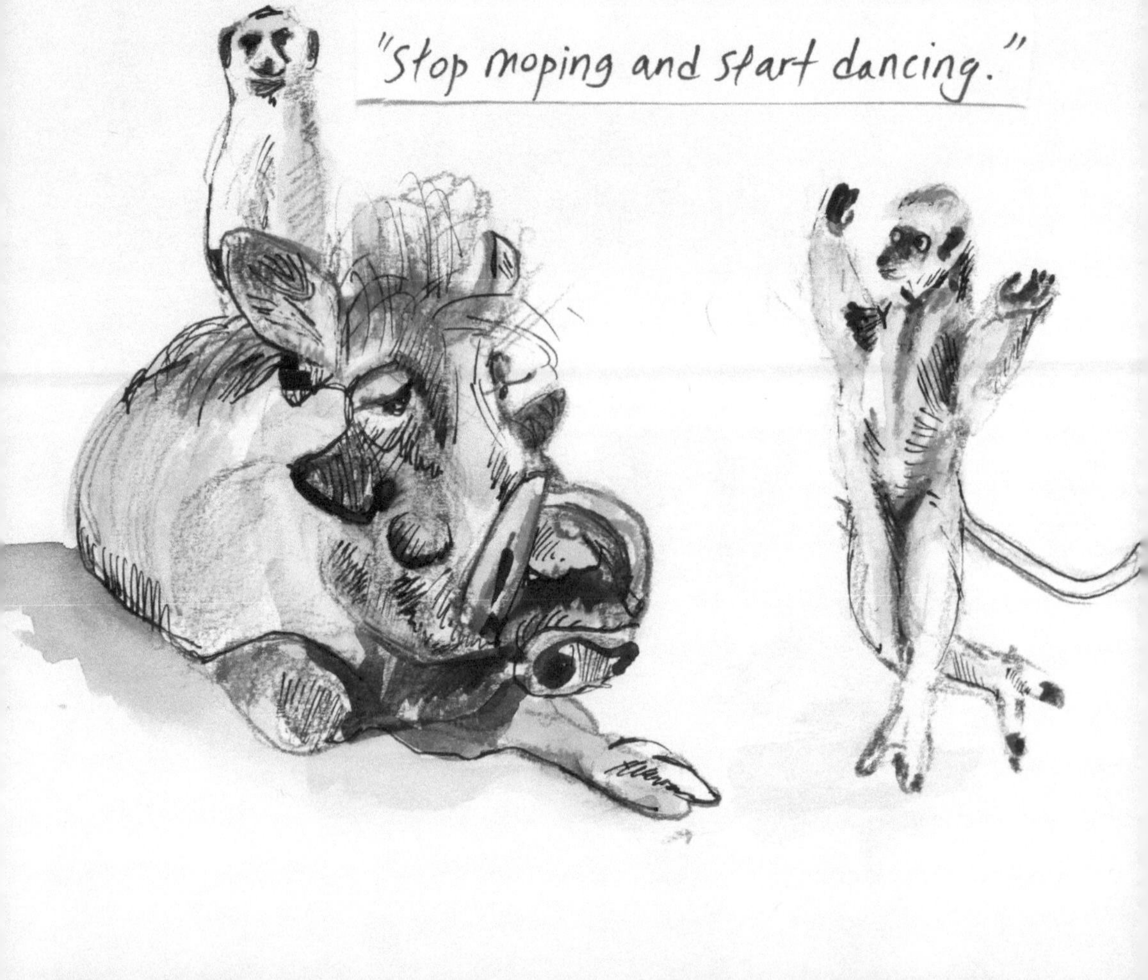

"Stop moping and start dancing."

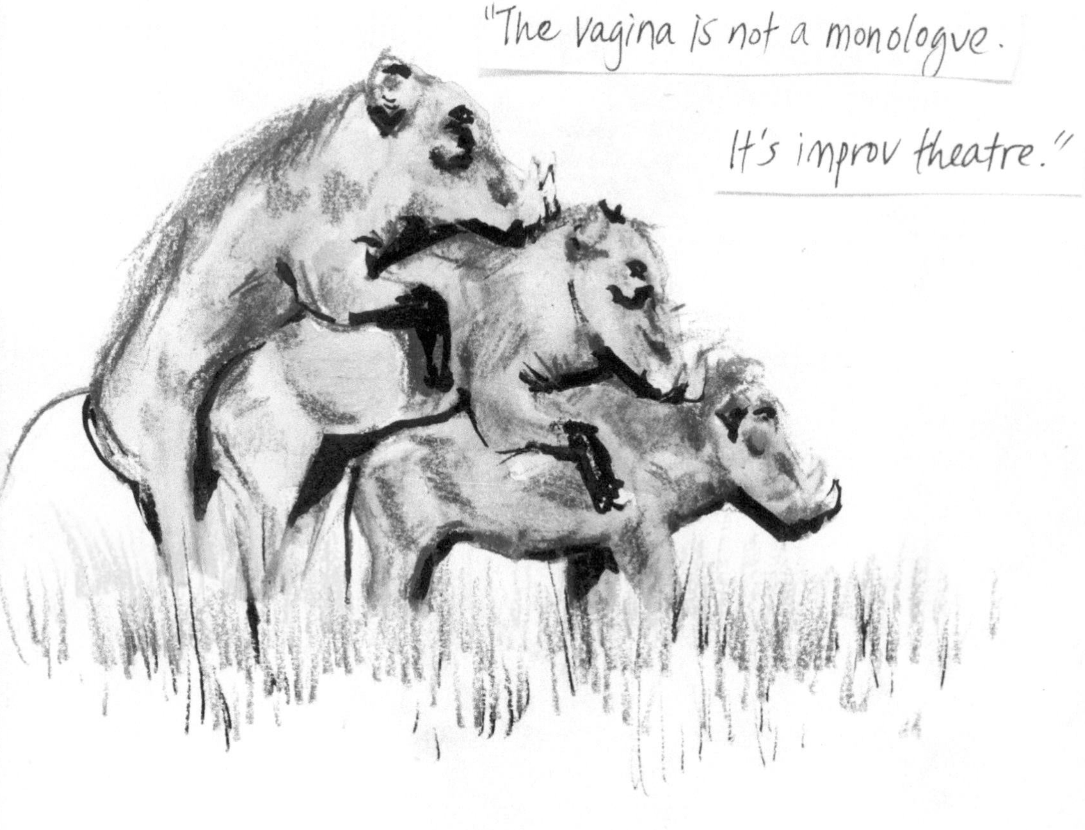
"The vagina is not a monologue.
It's improv theatre."

"Marriage isn't an answer.

It's a whole new set of questions."

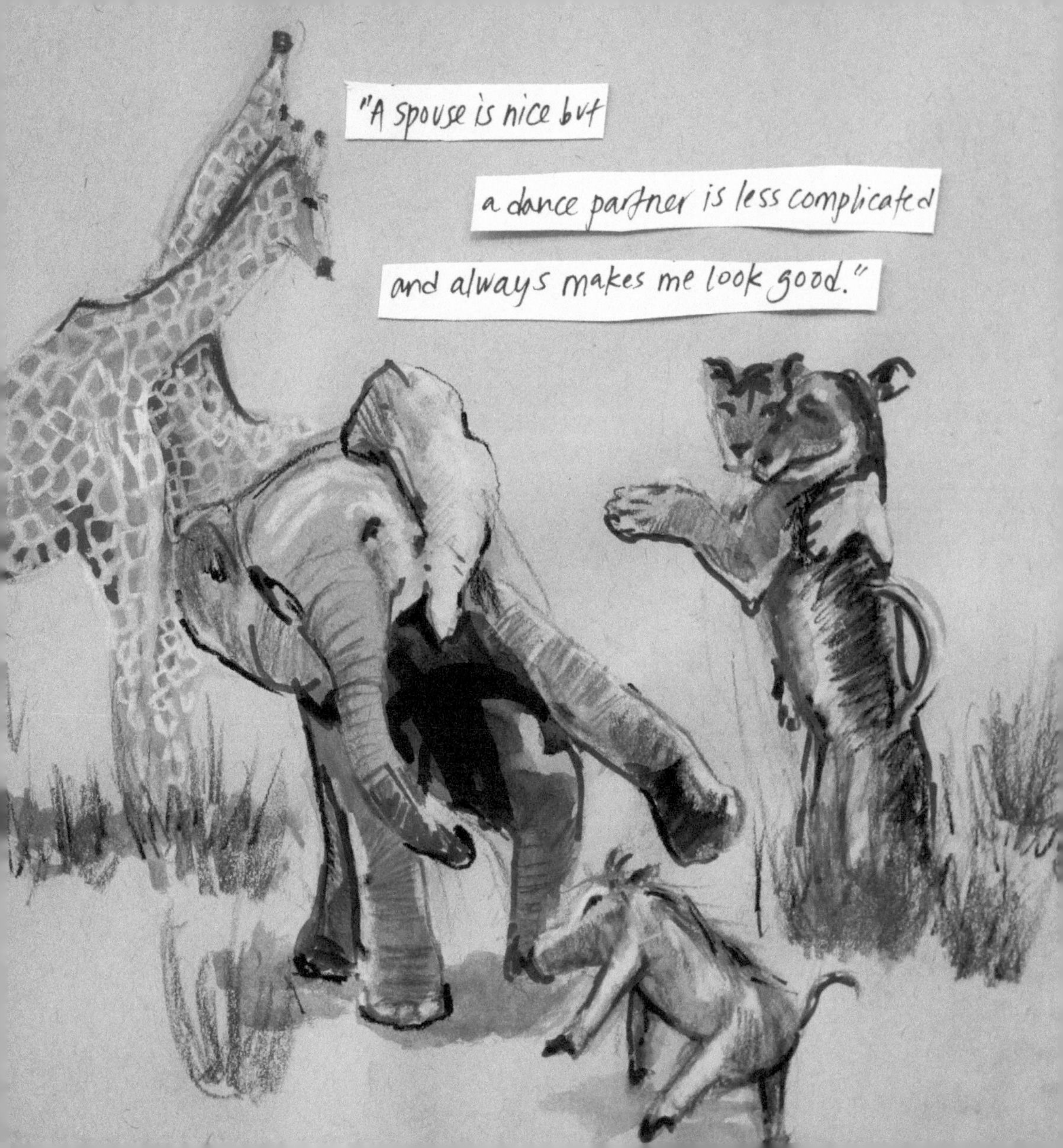
"A spouse is nice but
a dance partner is less complicated
and always makes me look good."

"Love later in life is sags, bags, hugs & kisses".

"When whispering sweet nothings
in my lover's ear,
I make sure
it's the good one."

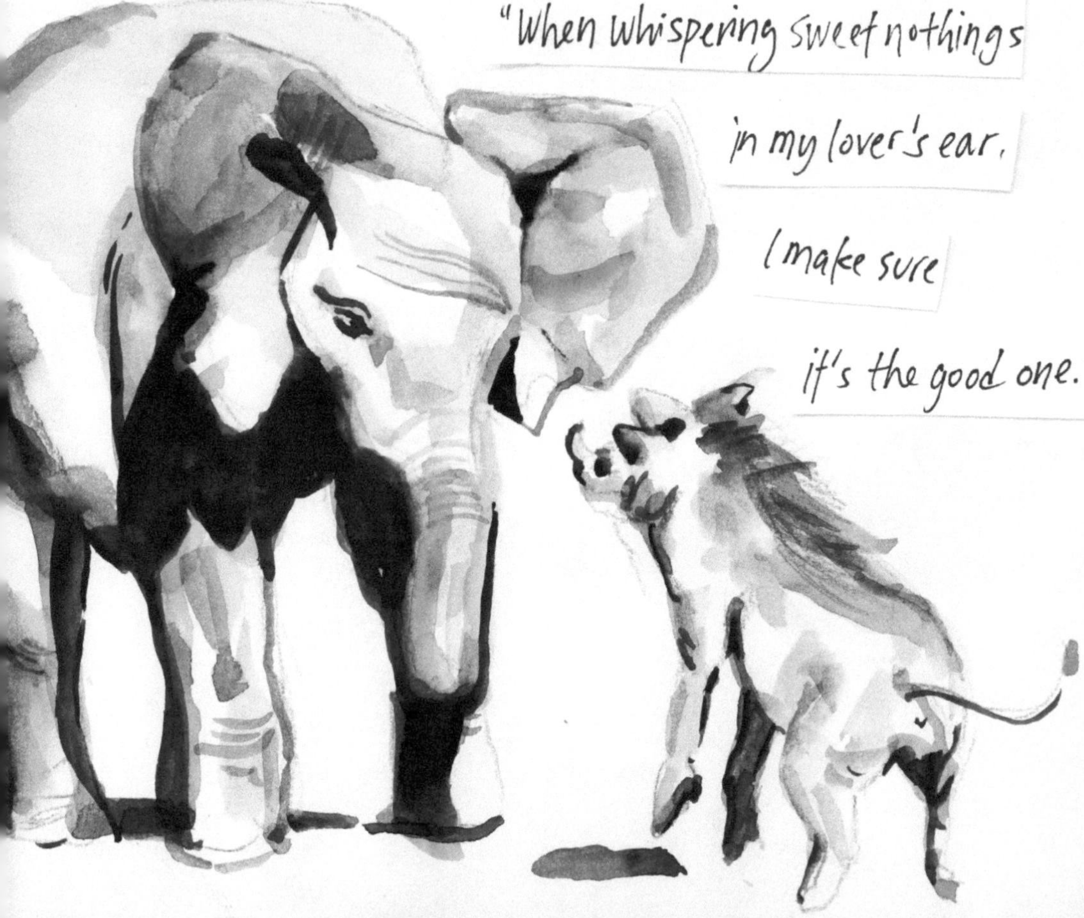

On Crises

What Next?

My husband had been a well-known newspaper columnist and was passionate in his conviction that a high-quality education was the key to breaking the poverty-to-prison pipeline. Only 11 months after Russell died, my children Alison and Russell Jr. and I founded the Russell Byers Charter School.

From the day our application was approved by the Board of Education, we had only seven months to find a building, hire a principal and teachers, create a curriculum, recruit students, buy furniture and get it all up and running. Our doors opened on September 11th, 2001.

Wait... 9/11?

You've got to be kidding.

120 students between four and seven years old arrived on time from across the city. On the first day of school we had to put our emergency plan into effect. Who would have thought?

And it worked!

Sometimes Plan B is really Plan A.

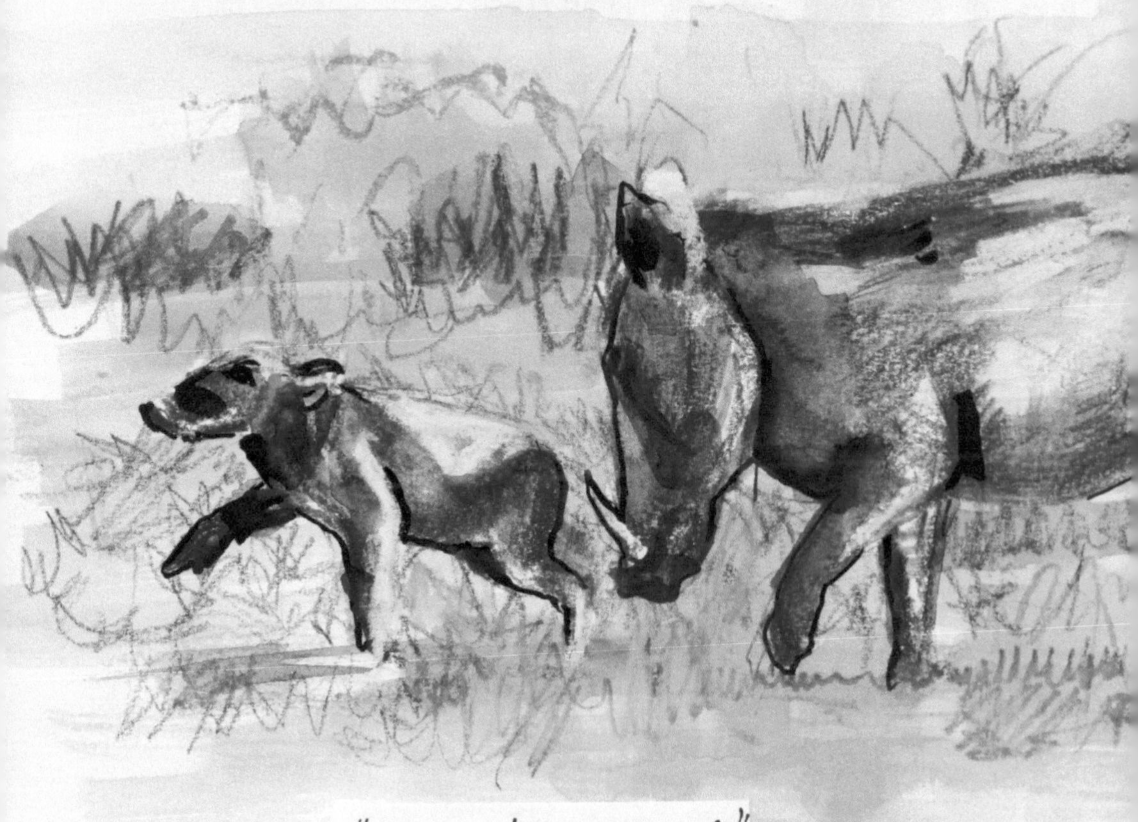

"Sweat the small stuff."

"Wisdom is earned."

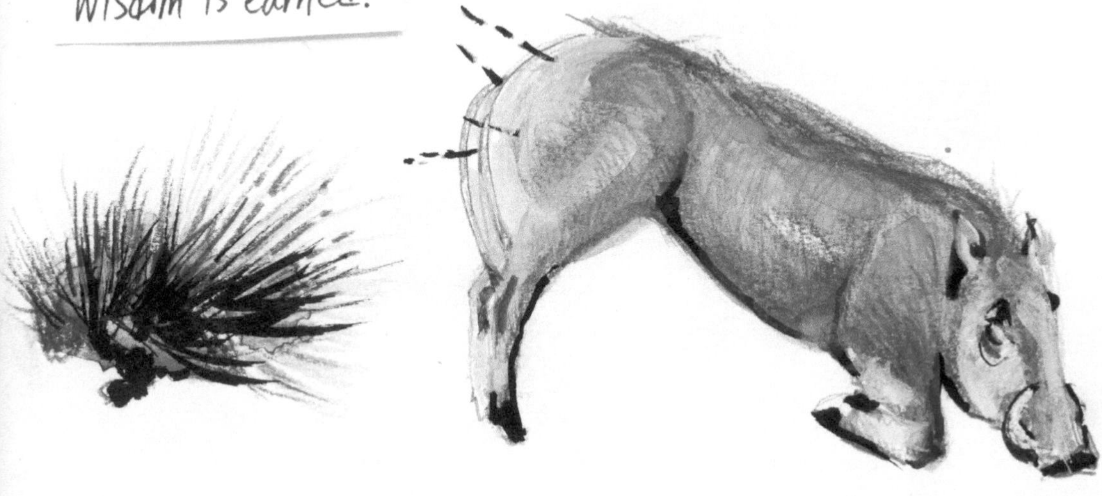

"Sometimes, there never was a 'Plan A'."

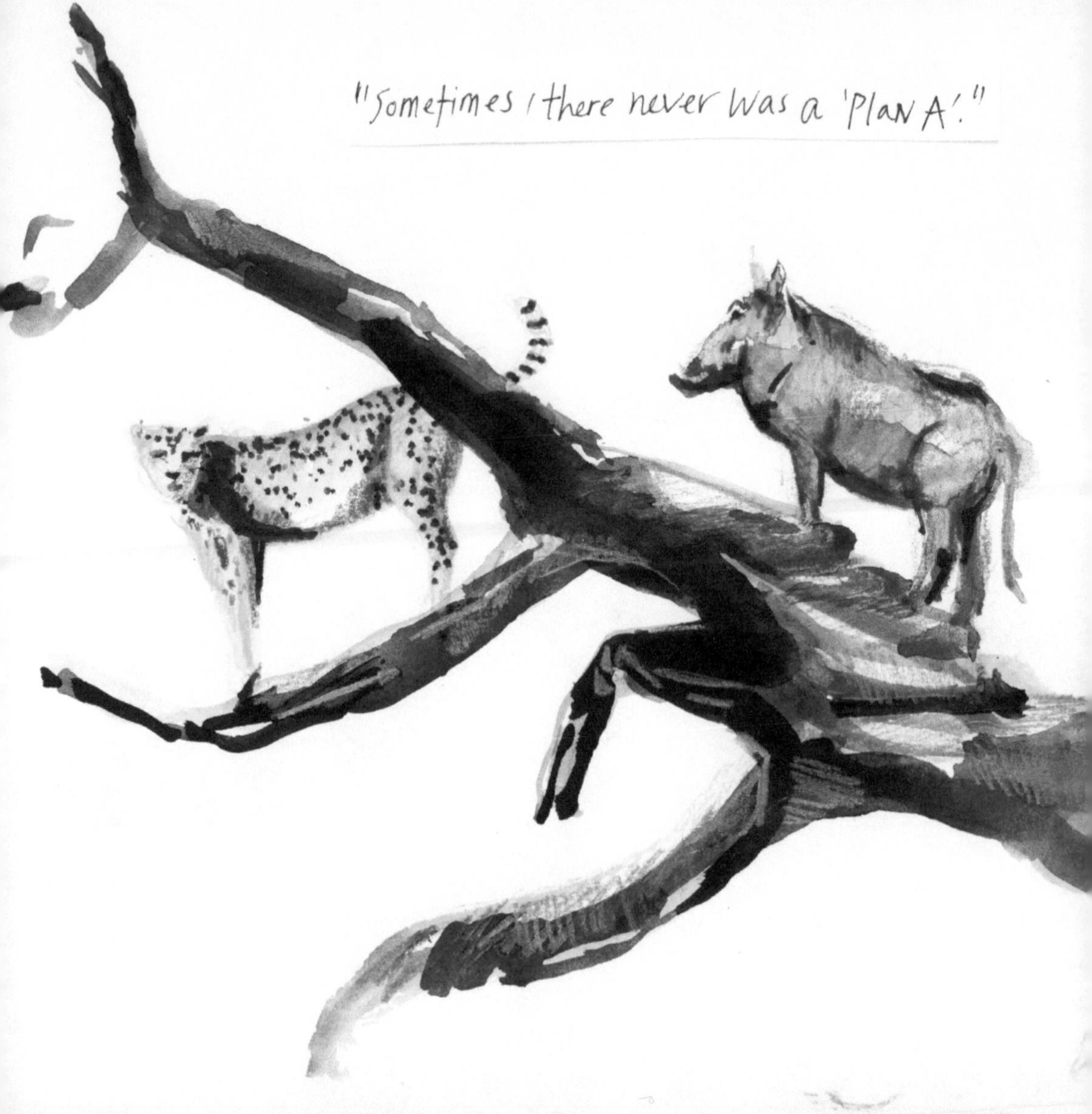

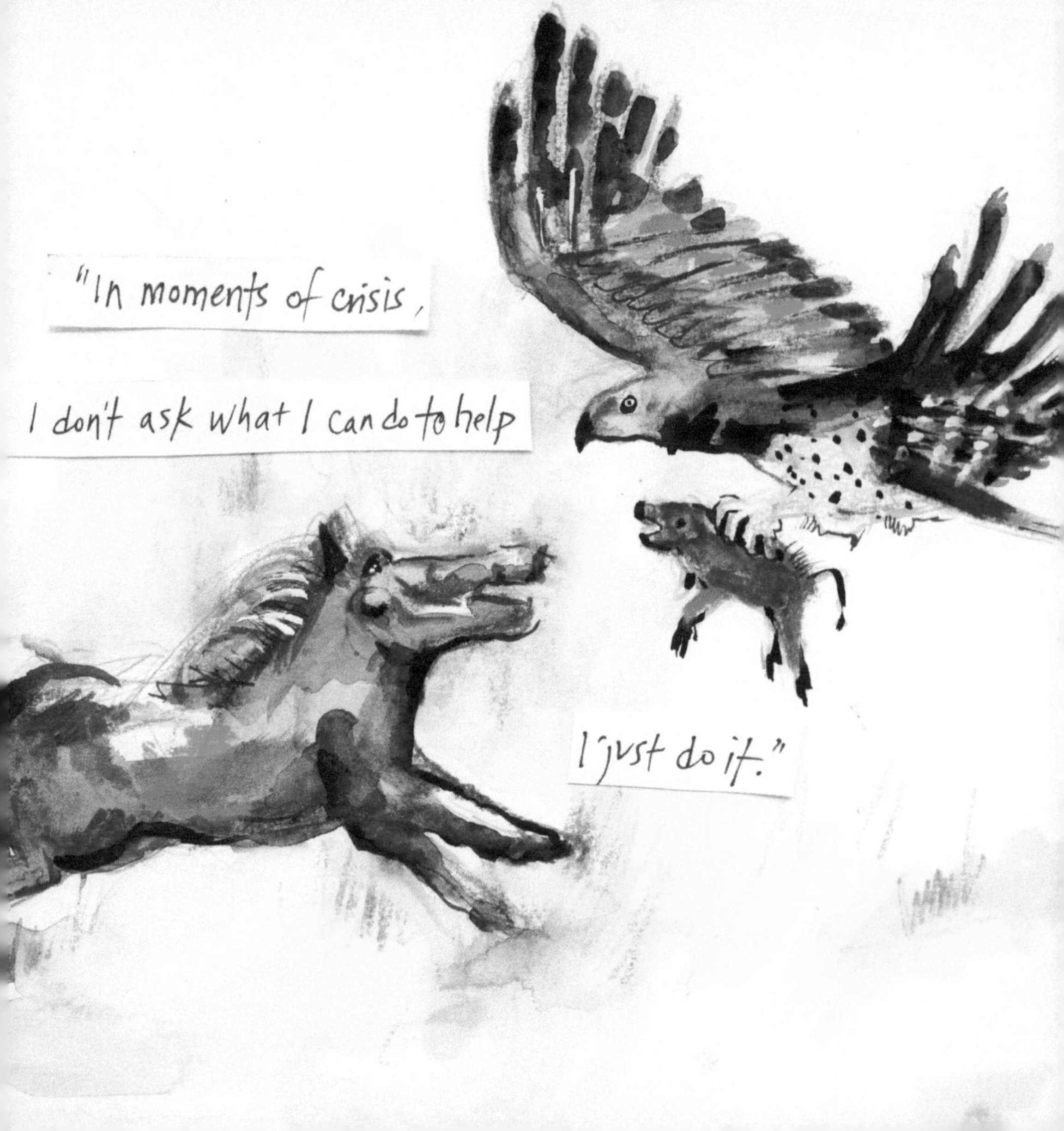
"In moments of crisis,
I don't ask what I can do to help
I just do it."

"Power is keeping the ball
in someone else's court.

Bullying is holding onto the ball
until the whole game stops."

"living life 'yes and'

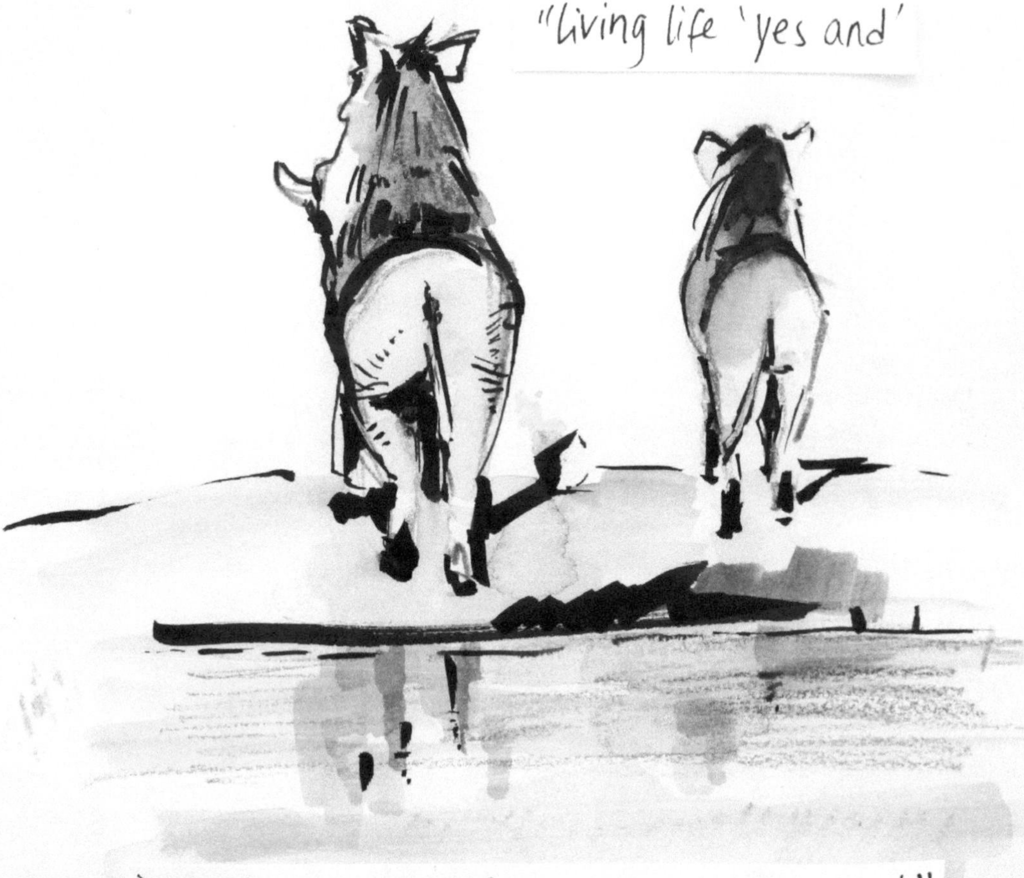

is much more satisfying than 'yes, but...'"

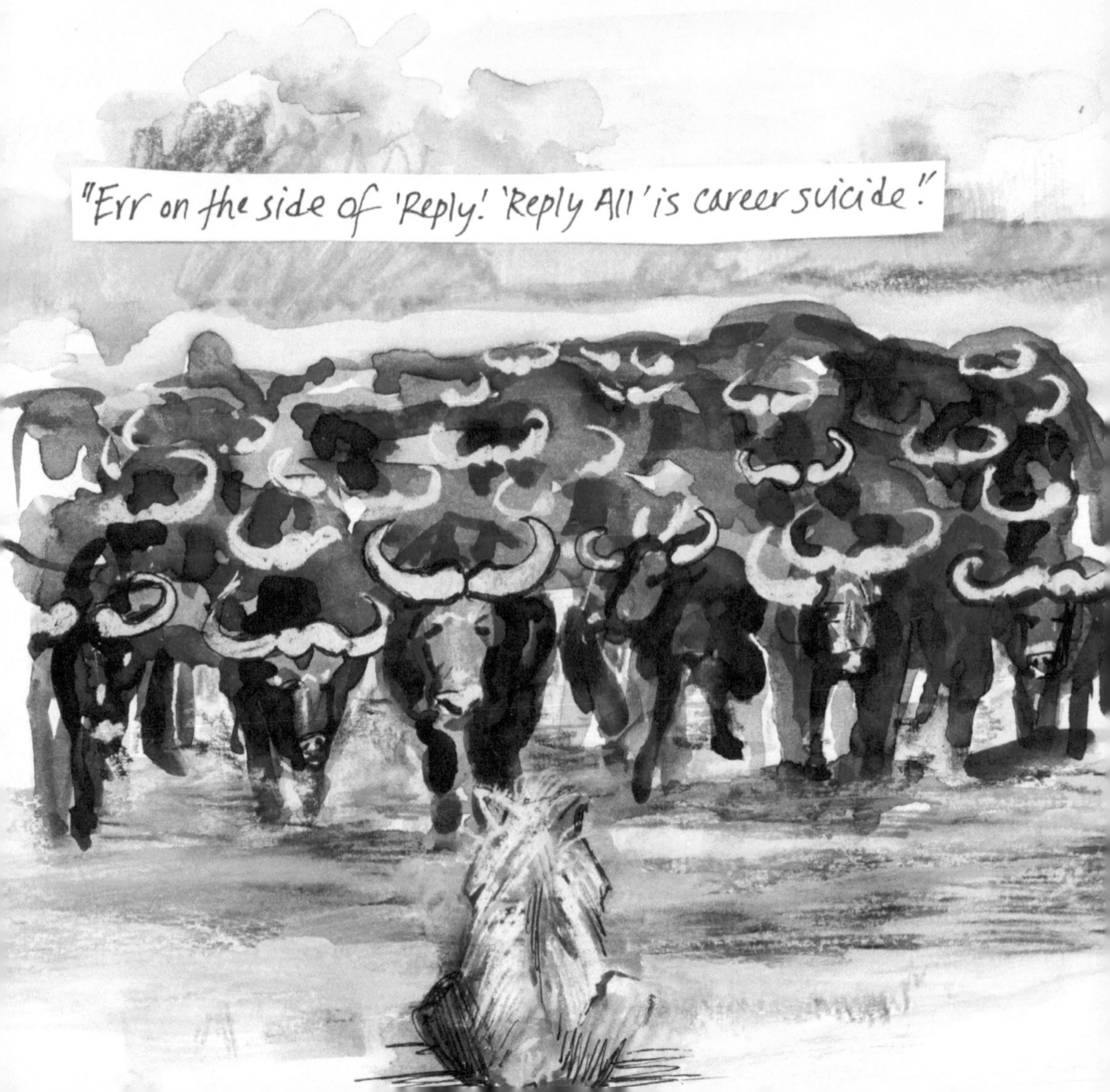
"Err on the side of 'Reply.' 'Reply All' is career suicide."

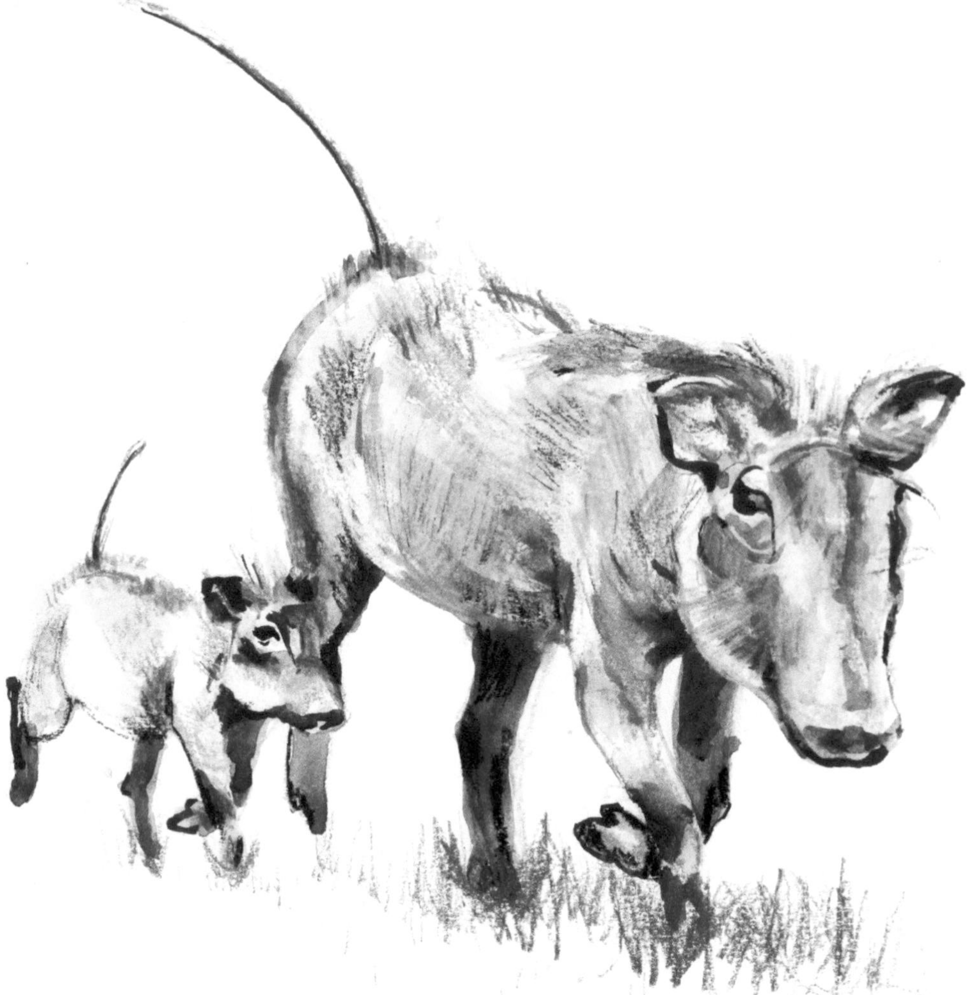

"A crew is always stronger than an individual."

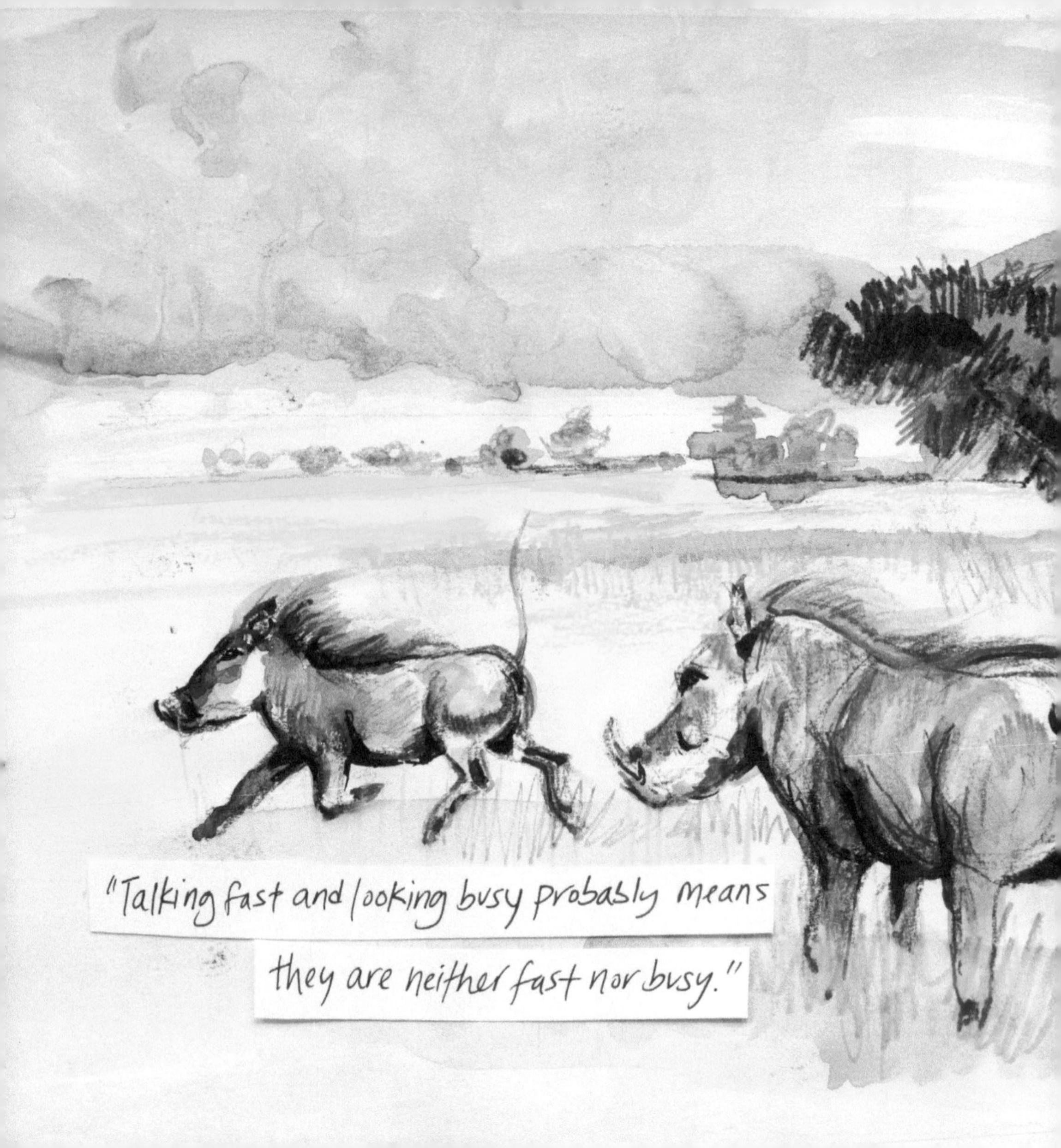
"Talking fast and looking busy probably means
they are neither fast nor busy."

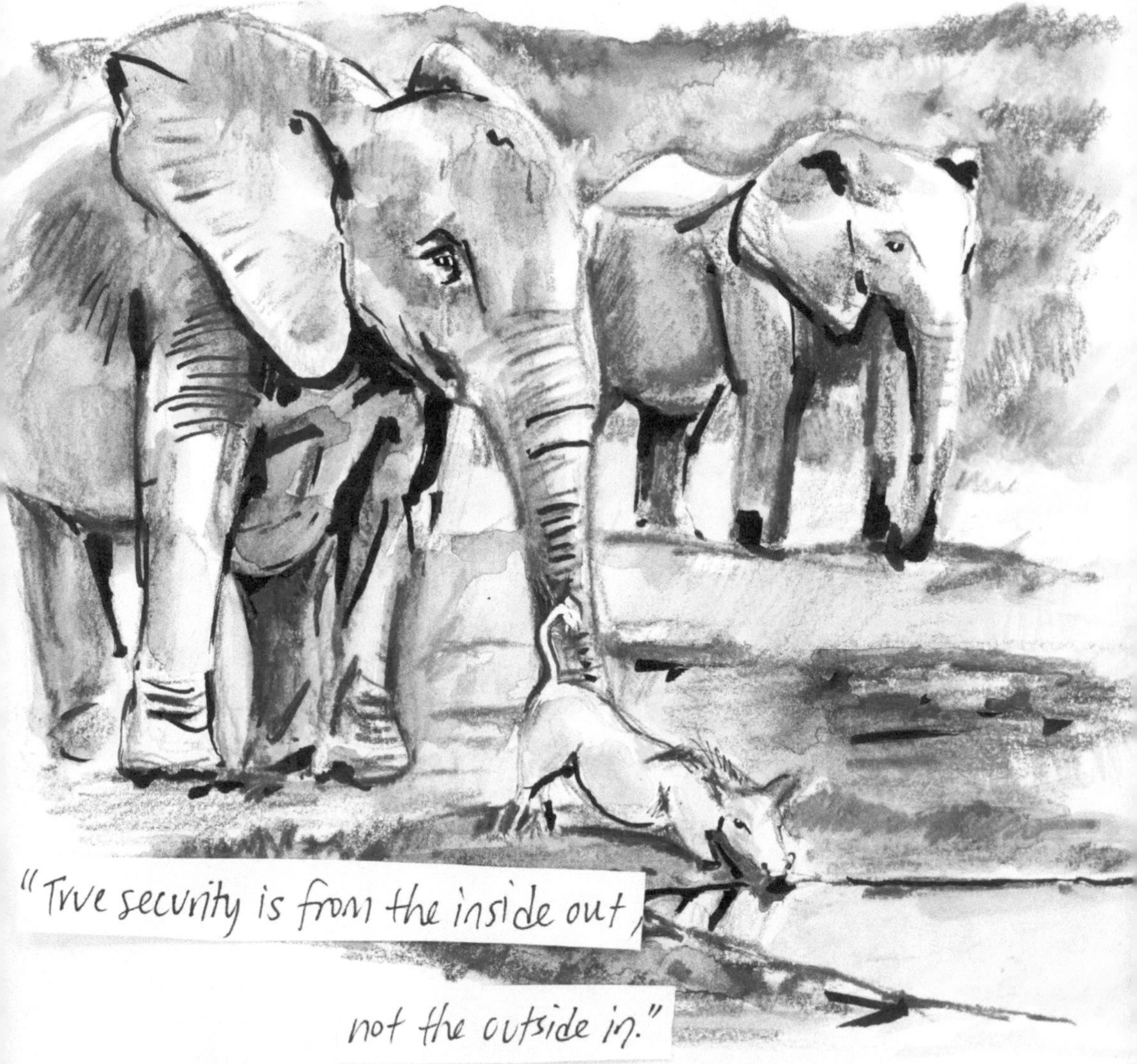
"True security is from the inside out,
not the outside in."

On Health

When is Enough Enough?

In the fall of 2009, I noticed a mild tremor in my foot. Turns out it's Parkinson's Disease. How did this happen?
While a murderer can be put in prison, sickness, old age and death are always on the loose!
The thought of retiring early while Parkinson's got to work sounded very unappealing.

So, I didn't.

Three years later, before a much-anticipated family trip to Africa, the doctor called to inform me of some
abnormal test results. I decided to travel anyway and delay further testing until my return.
What's the point of prolonging life if you can't enjoy it? Not all medicine comes in a bottle.
The diagnosis was anal cancer. After chemo and six weeks of radiation, I was overjoyed to learn that I was cancer-free.

Apparently, my vagina's still downright angry about it. Who knew?!

Now into my ninth year of living with Parkinson's, I wake up every day feeling like the Tin Man.
There are days when my foot aches, shakes, and drags so obviously,
I have to remove my shoe to walk the hallways at Russell Byers.

Giving up a boot is one thing. Giving the boot to your life is another.

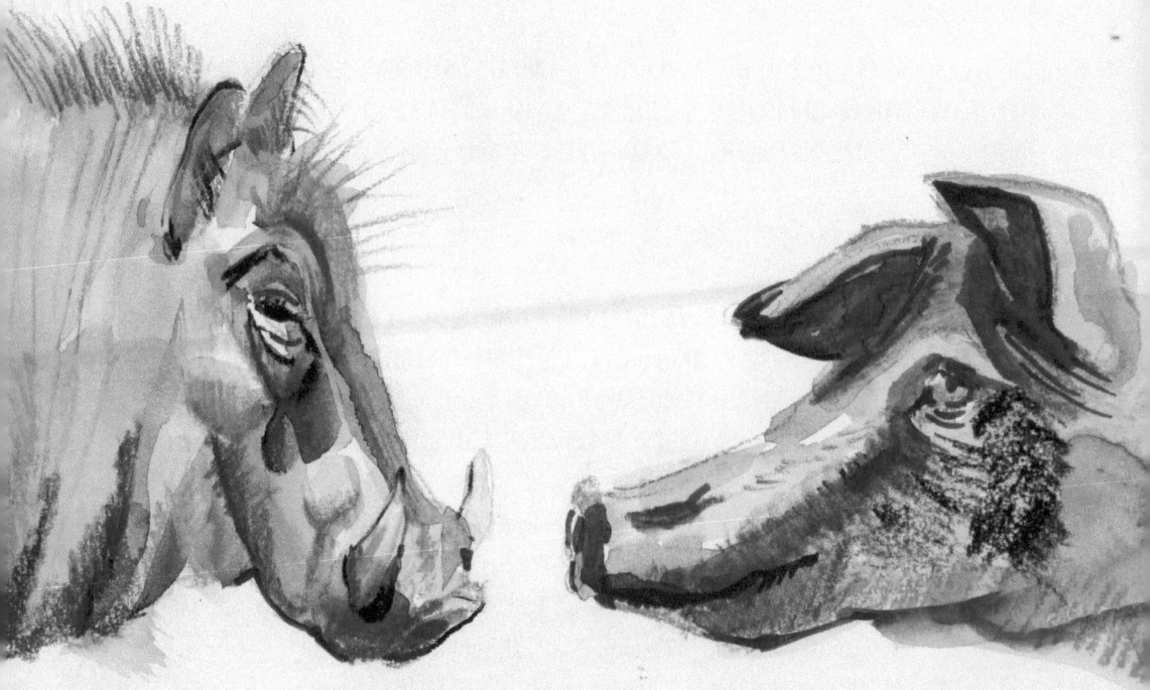

"plastic surgery is bad for the nervous system."

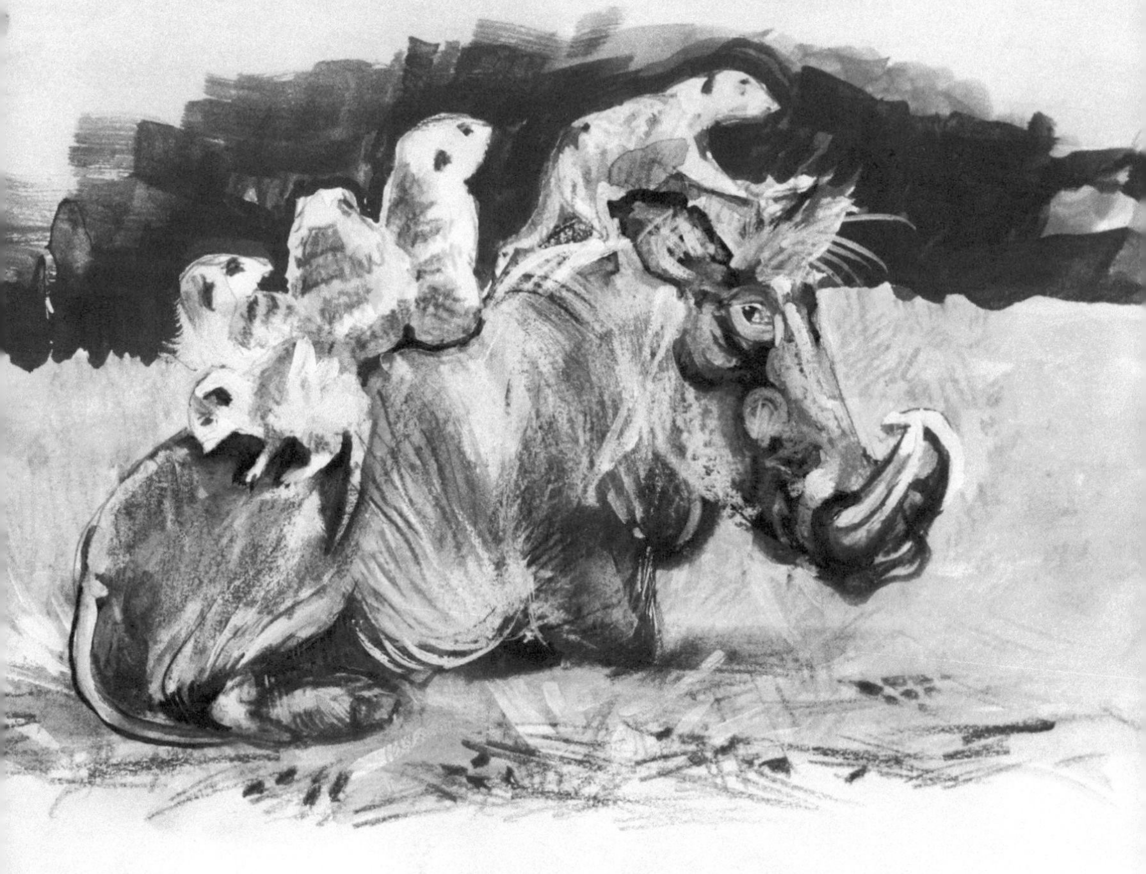

"Everything in moderation including moderation."

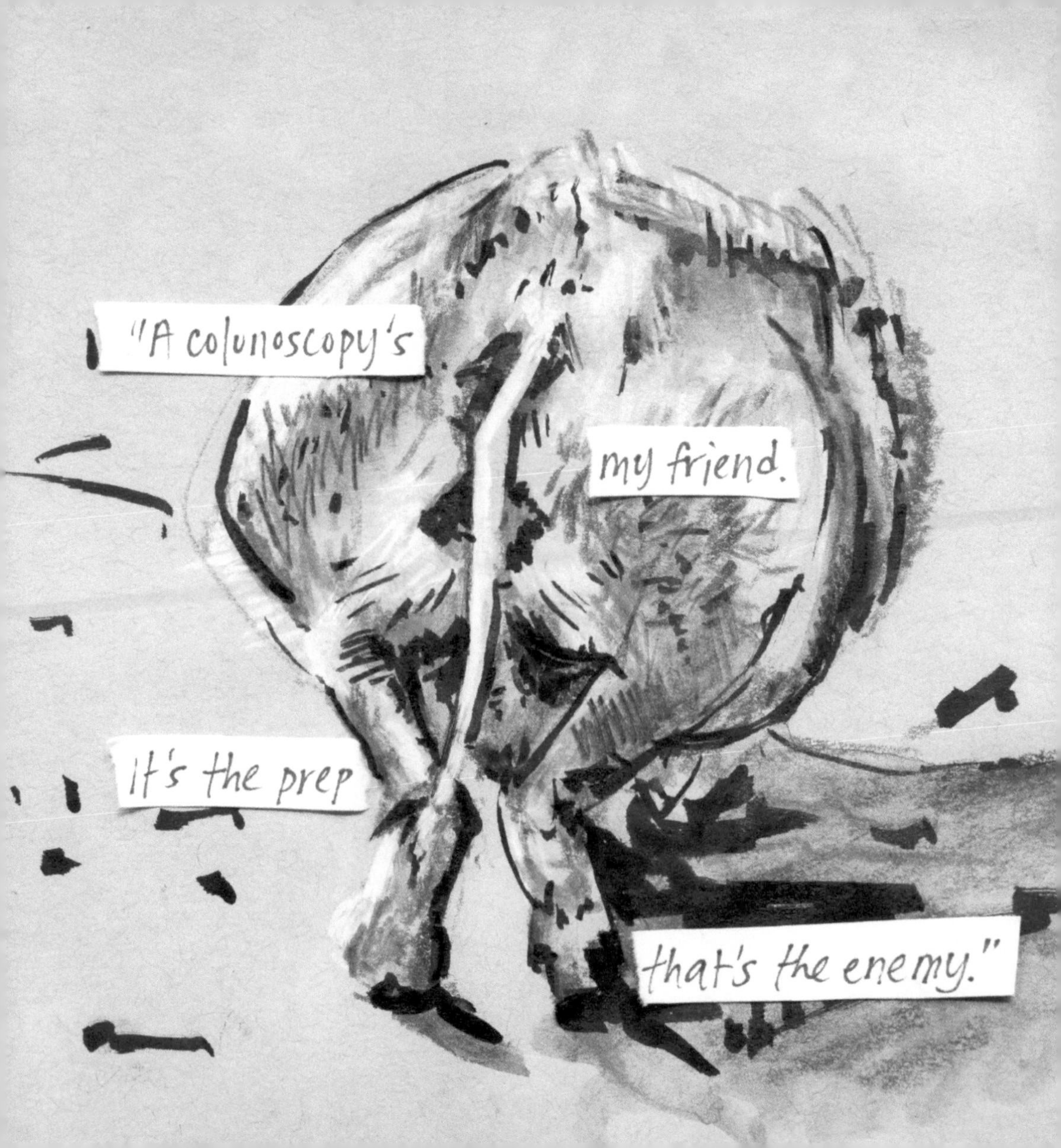
"A colonoscopy's
my friend.
It's the prep
that's the enemy."

"Nobody told me about cancer's collateral damage."

"Surviving isn't enough.

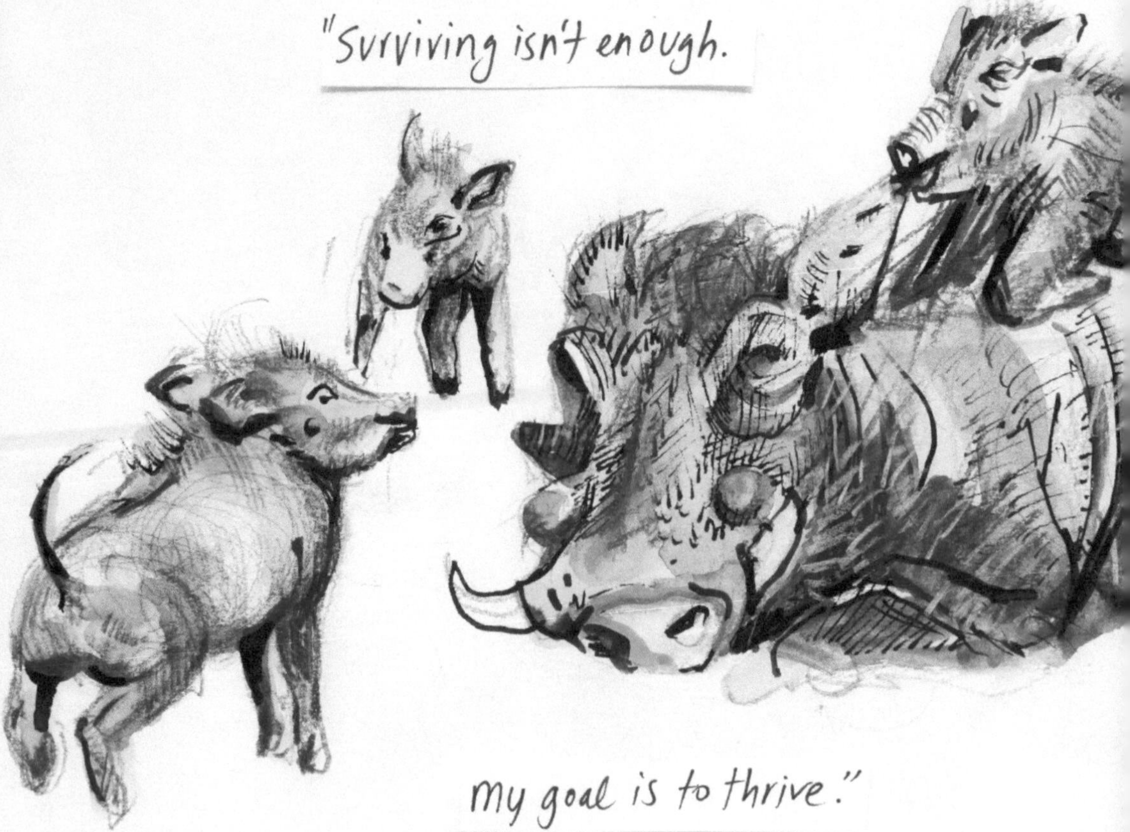

my goal is to thrive."

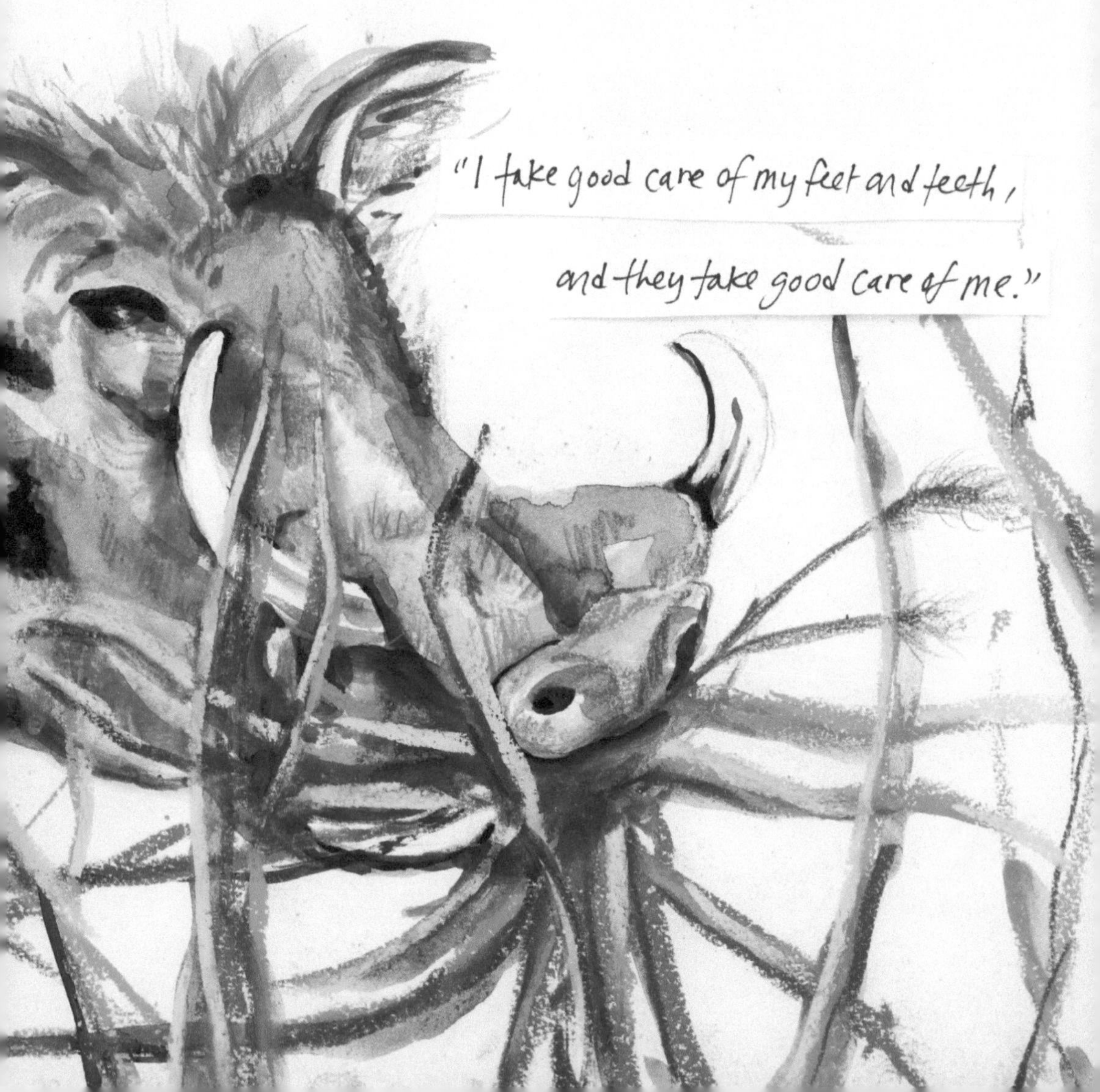
"I take good care of my feet and teeth,
and they take good care of me."

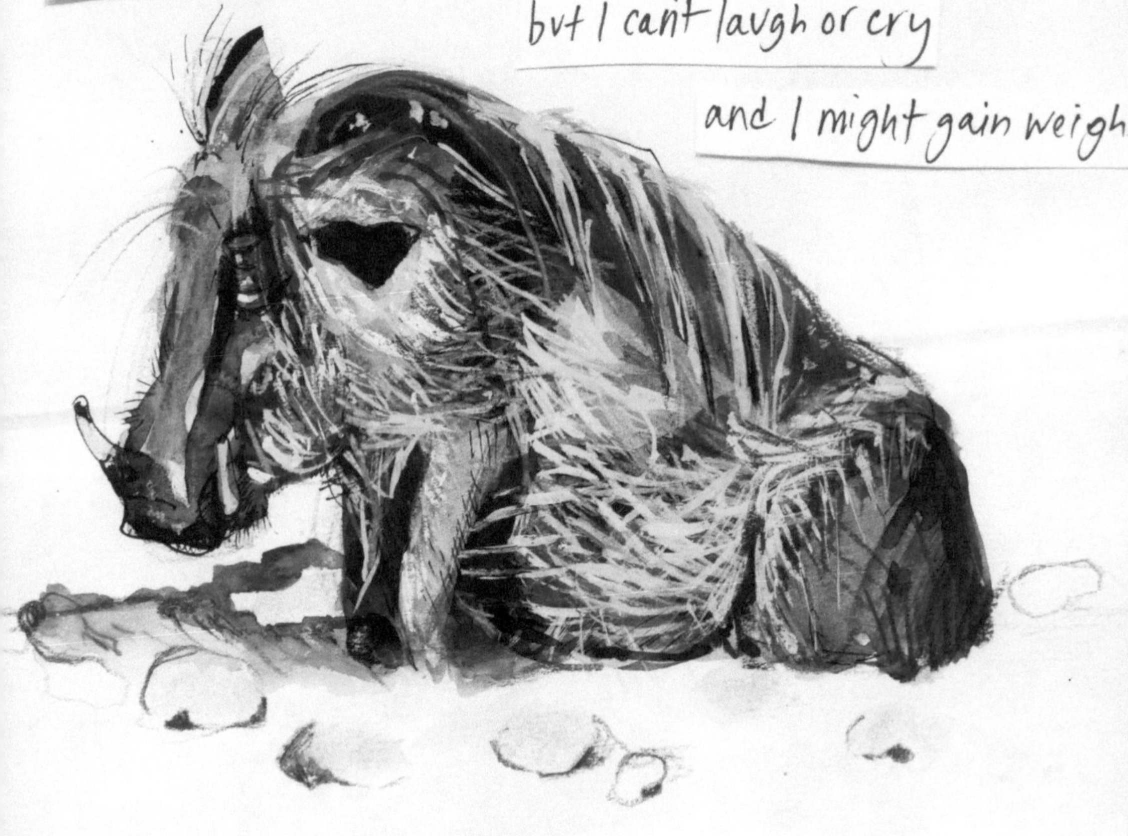
"Antidepressants may mask the pain,
but I can't laugh or cry
and I might gain weight
... so what's the point?"

"There is a brain in my gut.

Who knew?"

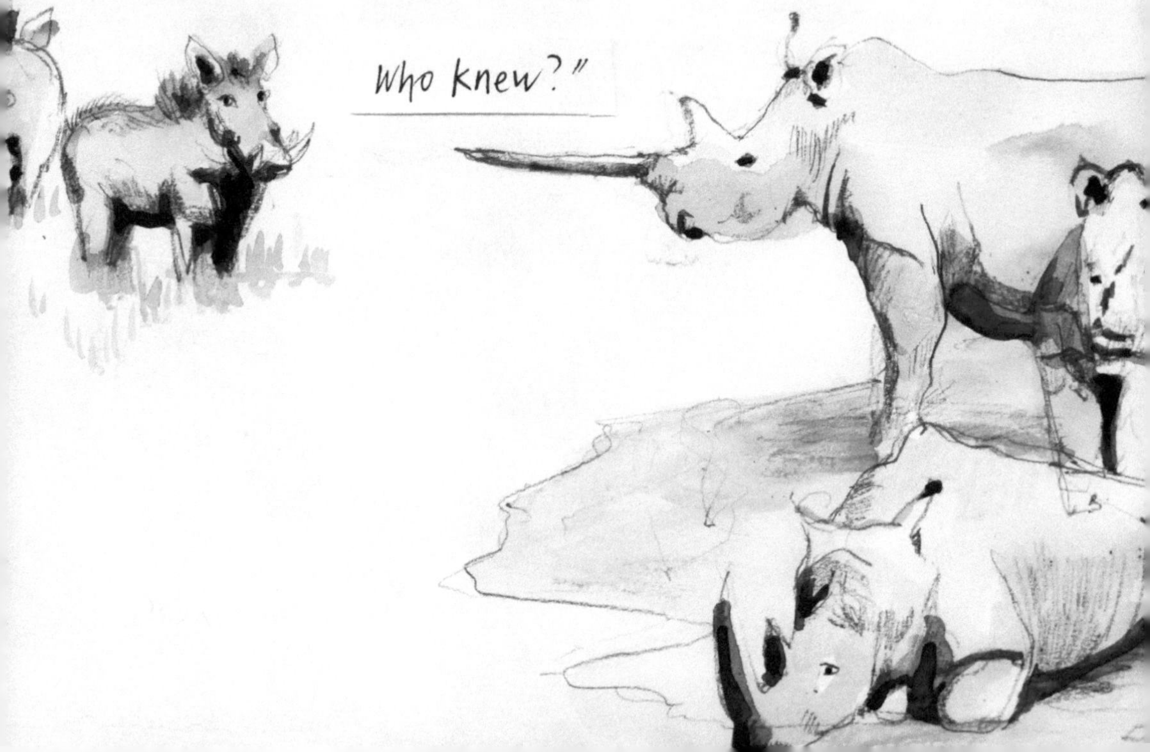

"I don't take any medicine

until I've read the

small print.

I learned the hard way."

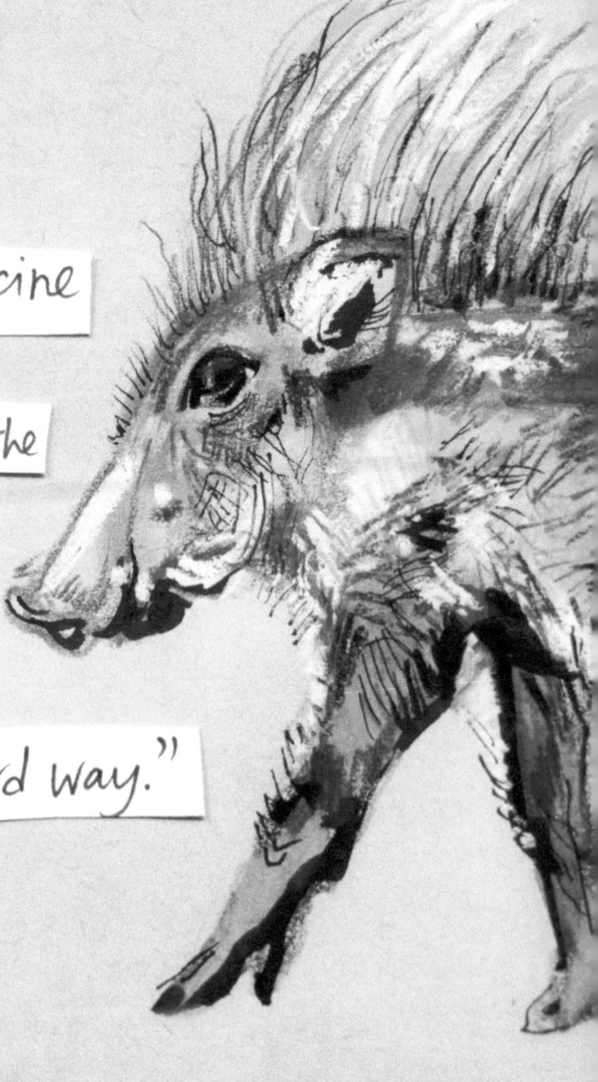

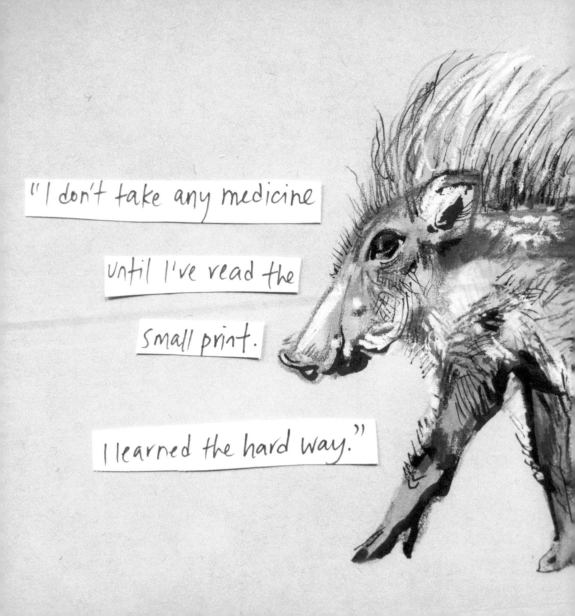

"Rosy cheeks

and cherry lips

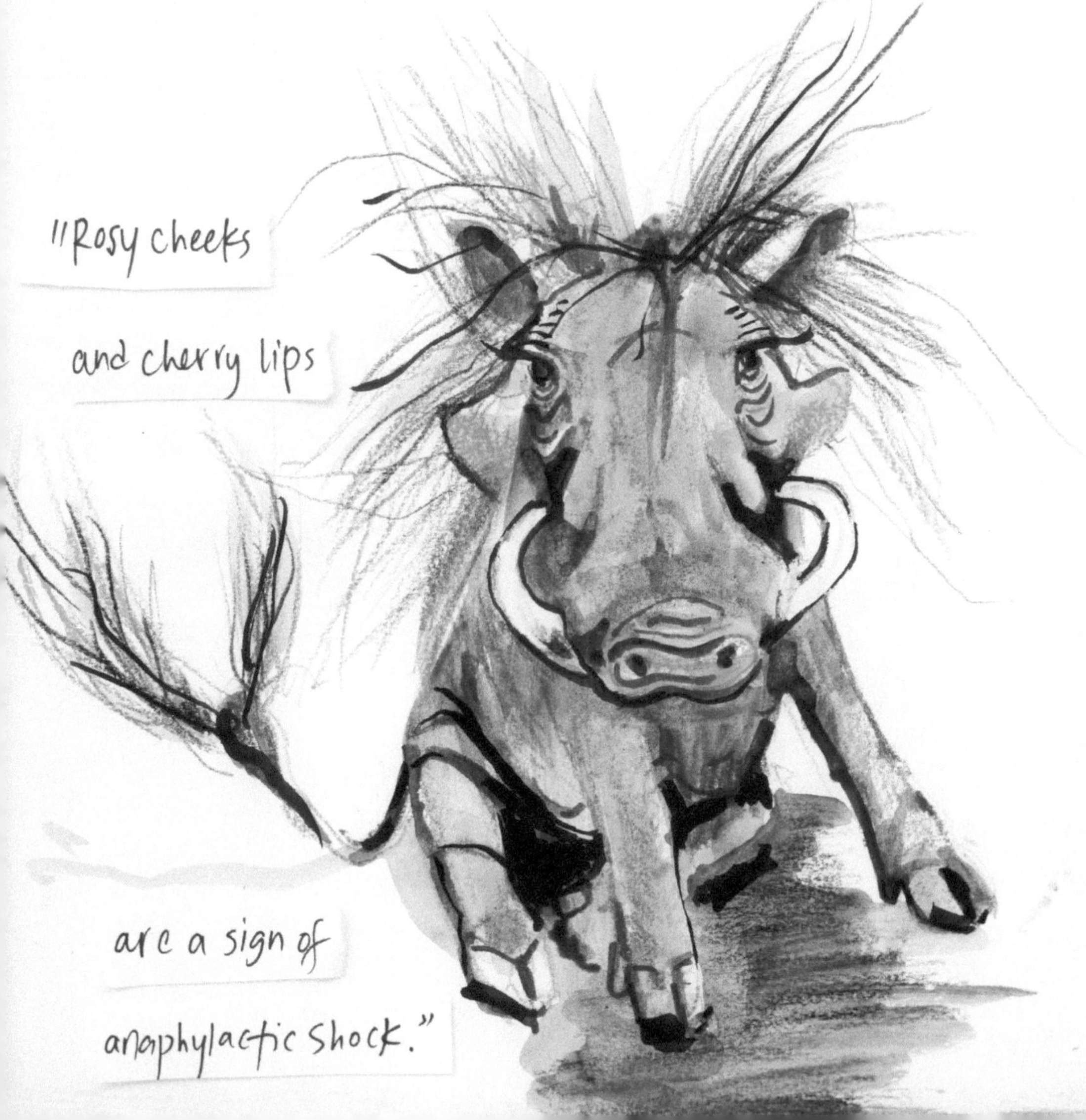

are a sign of

anaphylactic shock."

"Having Parkinson's is waking up every day

feeling like the Tin Man

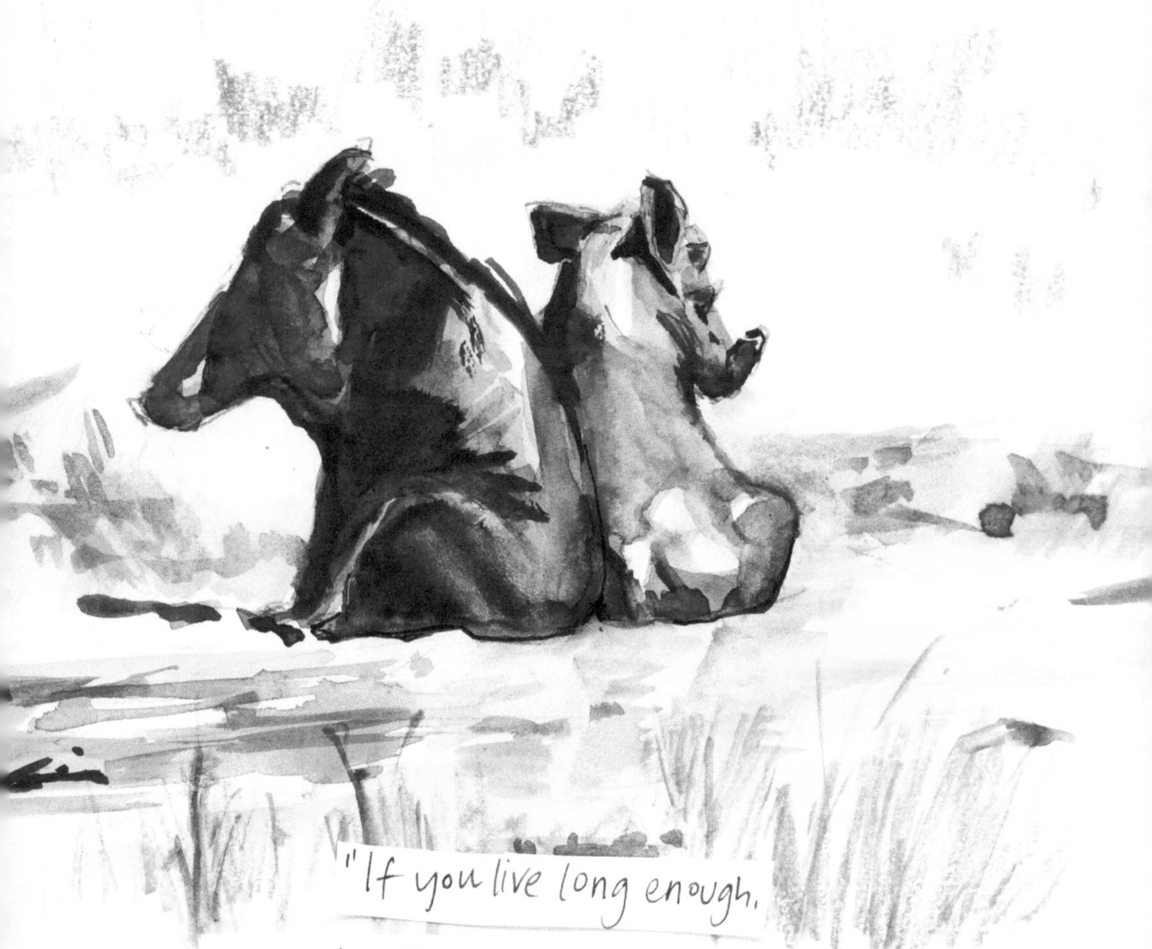

"If you live long enough,
unexpected things will begin to happen."

How am I?

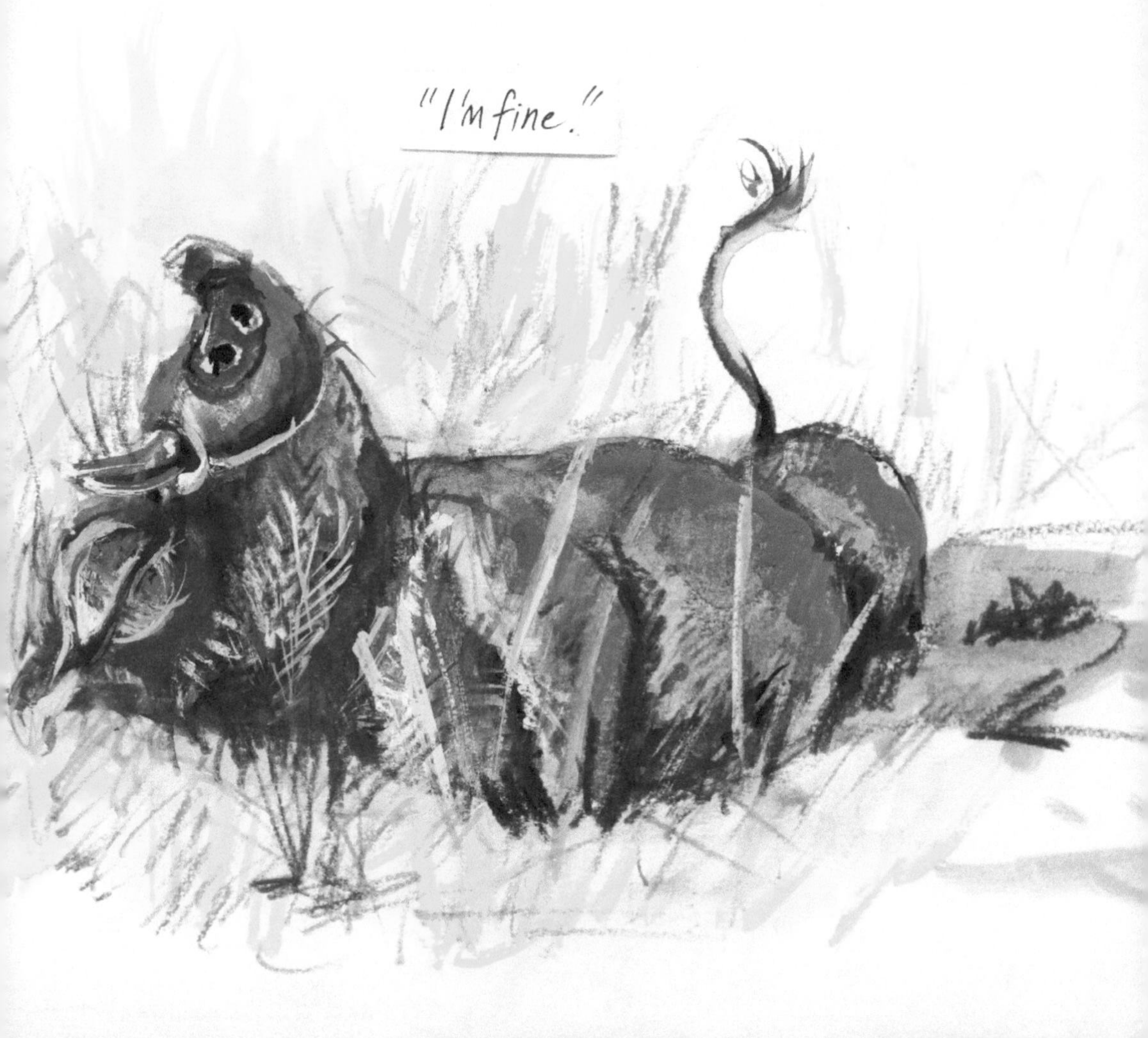
"I'm fine."

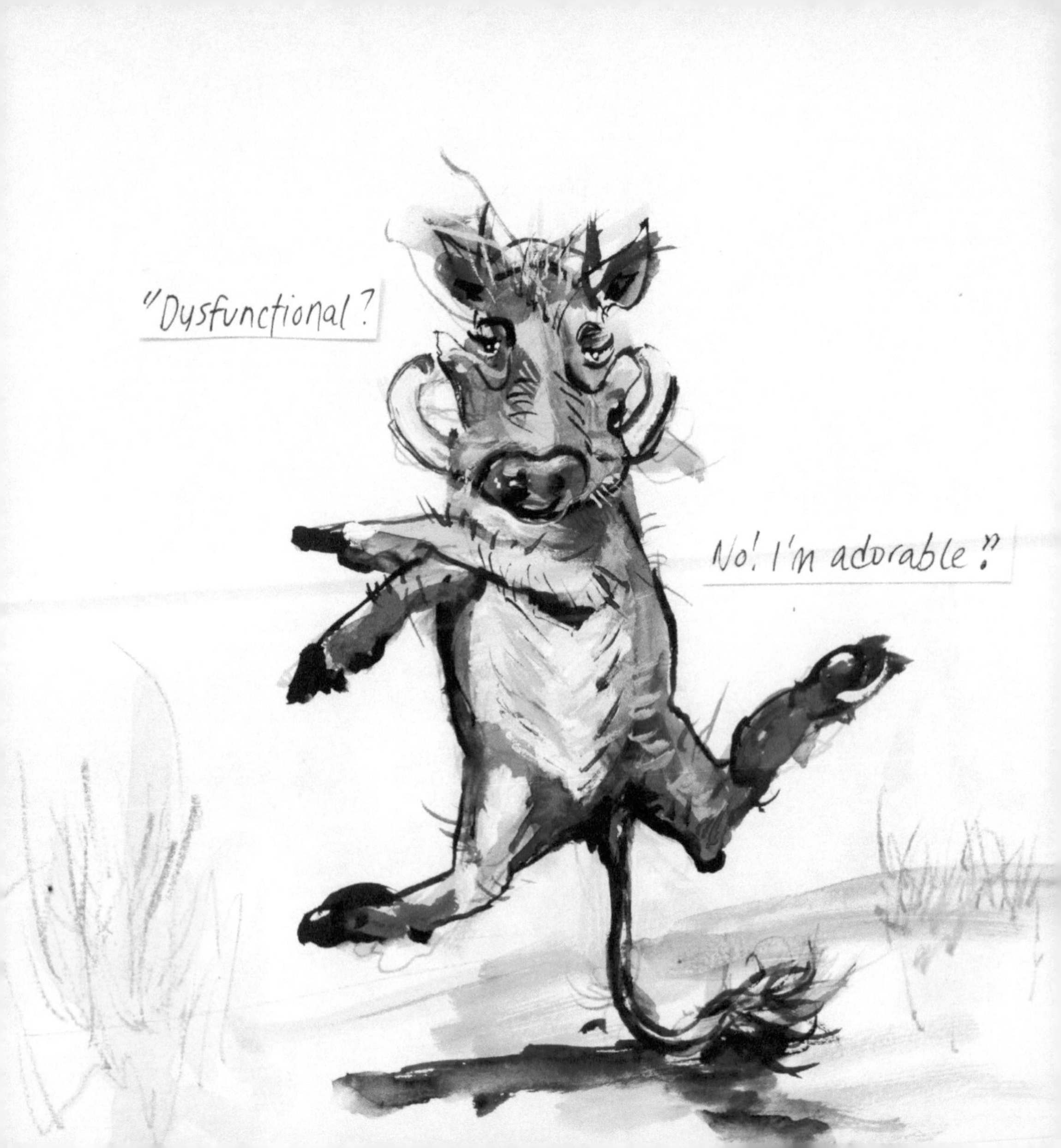
"Dysfunctional?
No! I'm adorable!"

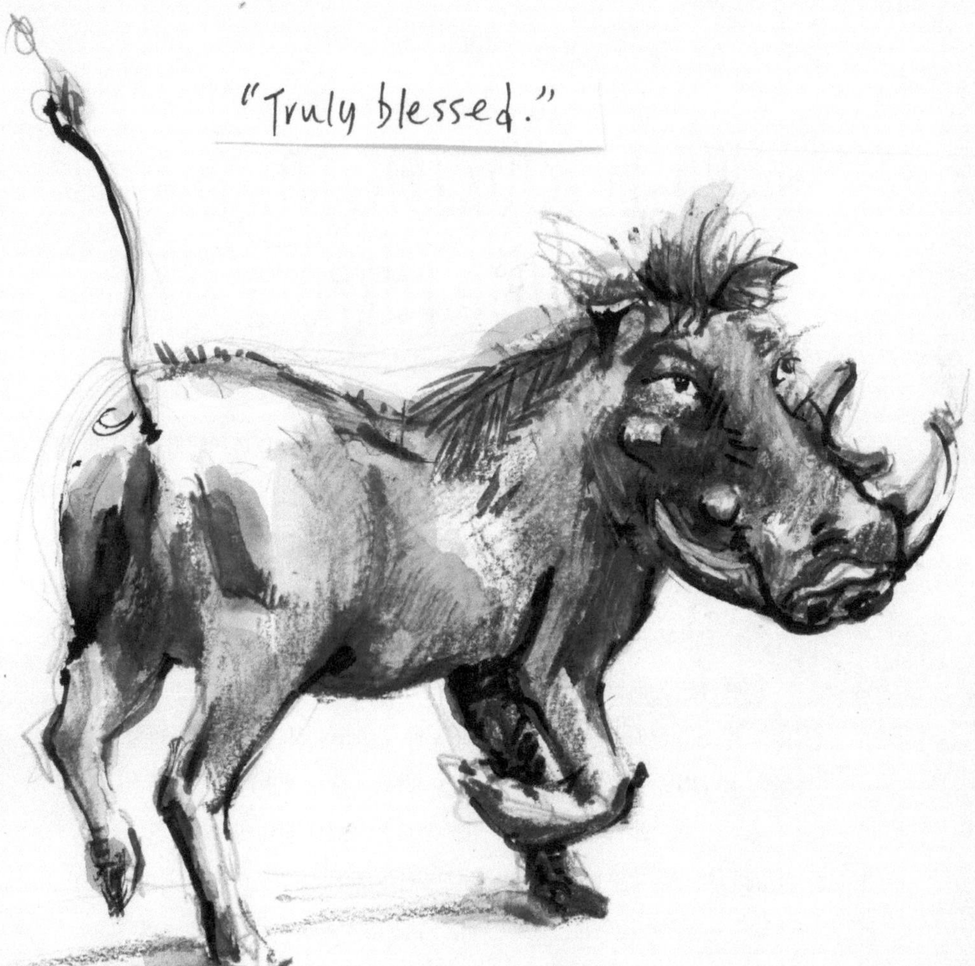
"Truly blessed."

"LIKE A WARTHOG, MY LIFE ISN'T PERFECT BUT IT'S FULL OF PURPOSE AND PROMISE AND THAT'S MORE THAN ENOUGH"

While looking for peace
I found purpose...

My collaborator Natalie — I can't imagine a more glorious partner for this warthog of a tale.

My father Brand, who gave me yellow legal pads to get organized and

My mother Bessie whose motto was "Only boring people get bored."

My husband Russell, who always had an opinion and expressed it...I miss you so much.

My children Russell and Alison, who kept me close during tough times

My grandchildren Russell III, Frick and Zander — who will you become?

My brother Brand and sister Adelaide, who gave me keys to their homes

My fantastic in-laws Anne, Jack, Becky, Carol, Monty, Mia and Mick

My oldest friend Judee, who is always there for me

My true friend Caroline, who was in the trenches with me for seven years to ensure there would be a

Russell Byers Charter School

My Parkinson's confidant Jonathan

My Comfort Aleyda

My Attack Quaker Signe

My secret weapon Sandy

My design czarina Veronica

My grit friend Angela

My dance teacher Vuthy, who makes me feel like Ginger Rogers

My fearless lawyer Carolyn

My Little Book of Blessings collaborator, Joe

My shrinks, who never gave up...whom I left...I really was listening

My Pickle Mafia — those on earth and in heaven

My Wellness Gurus, Andrea, George, Joy, Patty, Anna, Erica, Beth and Louis - who keep me upright every day

My right hand and my left hand, Debbie and Vanessa, who have kept me out of trouble

My Mr. — you know who you are — bringing me joy

My Philadelphia Charter School Warriors...and all the loyal donors who support us

And, of course, all the students, families, faculty, staff, board members and contributors to the

Russell Byers Charter School— past, present and future

...I am forever grateful.

What's your wild wisdom?

_____

_____

_____

_____

_____

_____

_____

_____

_____

_____

_____

_____

_____

_____

_____

_____

_____

_____

_____

_____

_____

_____

_____

_____

_____

_____

_____

_____

_____

_____

_____

_____

_____

_____

_____

_____

_____

_____

SHARE IT WITH US! WARTHOGPRODUCTIONS.COM

WARTHOG
PRODUCTIONS

CPSIA information can be obtained
at www.ICGtesting.com
Printed in the USA
BVHW020937110220
572025BV00001B/7